THE SMUGGLER:

A Tale.

BY G. P. R. JAMES, ESQ.

AUTHOR OF

"DARNLEY," "DE L'ORME," "RICHELIEU,"

ETC. ETC.

IN THREE VOLUMES.

VOL. III.

LONDON:

SMITH, ELDER AND CO., 65, CORNHILL.

1845.

THE SMUGGLER.

CHAPTER I.

It was two o'clock when Sir Robert Croyland left his daughter, and Edith, with the aid of her maid, soon recovered from the swoon into which she had fallen. At first she hardly knew where she was, or what had taken place. All seemed strange to her; for she had never fainted before; and though she had more than once seen her sister in the state in which she herself had just been, yet she did not apply what she had witnessed in others to explain her own sensations.

When she could rise from the sofa, where her father had laid her, and thought and recollection returned, Edith's first inquiry was for Sir Robert; and the servant's answer that he had been gone a quarter of an hour, was at first a relief. But Edith sat and pondered for a while, applying herself to call to mind all the last words which had been spoken. As she did so, a fear came over her—a fear that her meaning might have been mistaken. "No!" she murmured, at length—"no! I said, *but*—he must have heard it.—I cannot break those vows—I dare not; I would do anything to save him—oh, yes, doom myself to wretchedness for life; but I cannot, unless Henry gives me back my promise.—Poor Henry! what right have I to make him suffer too?—Yet does he suffer?—But a father's life—a father's life! That must not be the sacrifice!—Leave me, Caroline—I am better now!" she continued aloud; "it is very foolish to faint in this way. It never happened to me before."

"Oh dear, Miss Edith! it happens to every one now and then," said the maid, who had been in her service long; "and I am sure all Sir Robert said to you to-day, was enough to make you."

"Good heaven!" cried Edith; in alarm, "did you hear?"

"I could not help hearing a part, Miss Edith," answered the maid; "for in that little room, where I sit to be out of the way of all the black fellows, one hears very plain what is said here. There was once a door, I believe, and it is only just covered over."

For a moment, Edith sat mute in consternation; but at length demanded, "What did you hear? Tell me all, Caroline—every word, if you would ever have me regard you more."

"Oh, it was not much, Miss!" replied the maid; "I heard Sir Robert twice say, his life depended on it—and I suppose he meant, on your marrying young Mr. Radford. Then he seemed to tell you a long story; but I did not hear the whole of that; for I did not try, I can assure you, Miss Edith; and then I heard you say, 'To save you, my father, I would do anything—I *will* do anything, but—' and then you stopped in the middle, because I suppose you fainted."

Edith put her hands before her eyes and thought, or tried to think; for her ideas were still in sad confusion. "Leave me now, Caroline," she said; "but, remember, I expect that no part of any conversation you have overheard between me and my father, will ever be repeated."

"Oh dear, no, Miss Edith," replied the woman, "I would not on any account;" and she left the room.

We all know of what value are ordinary promises of secrecy, even in the best society, as it is called. Nine times out of ten, there is one dear friend to whom everything is revealed; and that dear friend has others; and at each remove, the bond of secrecy is weaker and more weak, till the whole world is made a hearer of the tale. Now Edith's maid was a very discreet person; and when she promised not to reveal what she had heard, she only proposed to herself, to tell it to one person in the world. Nor was that person her lover, or her friend, or her fellow-servant; nor was she moved by the spirit of gossip, but really and truly by a love for her young lady, which was great, and by a desire to serve her. Thus, she thought, as soon as she had shut the door, "I will tell it to Miss Zara, though; for it is but right that she should know how they are driving her sister to marry a man she hates, as well she may. Miss Zara is active and quick, and may find some means of helping her."

The maid had not been gone a minute, when she returned with the short note which Sir Robert Croyland had left; and as she handed it to her young mistress, she watched her countenance eagerly. But Edith took it, read it, and gazed upon the paper without a word.

"Pray, Miss Edith," said the maid, "are you likely to want me soon; for I wish to go up to the village for something?"

"No, Caroline—no," answered Edith, with an absent air; "I shall not want you;" and she remained standing with the paper in her hand, and her eyes fixed upon it.

The powers by which volition acts upon the mind, and in what volition really consists, are mysteries which have never yet, that I have seen, been explained. Yet certain it is, that there is something within us which, when the intellectual faculties seem, under the pressure of circumstances, to lose their functions, can by a great effort compel them to return to their duty, rally them, and array them, as it were, against the enemy by whom they have been routed. Edith Croyland made the effort, and succeeded. She had been taken by surprise, and overcome; but now she collected all the forces of her mind, and prepared to fight the battle over again. In a few minutes, she became calm, and applied herself to consider fully her own situation. There were filial duty and tenderness on one side—love and a strong vow on the other. "He has gone to tell Mr. Radford that I have consented," was her first distinct thought, "but his having mistaken me, must not make me give that consent when it is wrong. Were it myself alone, I would sacrifice all for him—I could but die—a few hours of misery are not much to bear—I have borne many. But I am bound—Good God! what an alternative!"

But I will not follow her thoughts: they can easily be conceived. She was left alone, with no one to counsel, with no one to aid her. The fatal secret she possessed was a bar to asking advice from any one. Buried in her own bosom, the causes of her conduct, the motives upon which she acted, must ever be secret, whatever course she pursued. Agony was on either hand. She had to choose between two terrible alternatives: on the one hand a breach of all her engagements, a few years, a few weeks, perhaps, of misery, and an early death—for such she knew must be her fate: and, on the other, a life, with love certainly to cheer it, but poisoned by the remembrance that she had sacrificed her father. Yet Edith now thought firmly, weighed, considered all.

She could come to no determination. Between two such gulfs, she shrank trembling from either.

The clock in the hall, with its clear, sharp bell, struck three; and the moment after, the quick sound of horses' feet was heard. "Can it be my father?" she thought. "No! he has not had time—unless he has doubted;" but while she asked herself the question, the horses stopped at the door, the bell rang; and she went on to say to herself, "perhaps it is Zara. That would be a comfort indeed, though I cannot tell her—I must not tell her all."

The old Hindoo opened the door, saying "Missy, a gentleman want to see you—very fine gentleman."

Edith could not speak; but she bowed her head, and the servant, receiving that token as assent, turned to some one behind him and said, "Walk in, sir."

For a moment or two, Edith did not raise her eyes, and her lips moved. She heard a step in the room, that made her heart flutter; she heard the door shut; but yet for an instant she remained with her head bent, and her hands clasped together. Then she looked up. Standing before her, and gazing intently upon her, was a tall handsome man, dressed in the splendid uniform of the dragoons of that time, and with a star upon his left breast—a decoration worn by persons who had the right to do so, more frequently in those days than at the present time. But it was to the face that Edith's eyes were turned—to the countenance well known and deeply loved. Changed though it was—grave where it had been gay, pale where it had been florid, sterner in the lines, once so full of gentle youth—still all the features were there, and the expression too, though saddened, was the same.

He gazed on her with a look full of tenderness and love; and their eyes met. On both of them the feelings of other years seemed to rush with overpowering force. The interval which had since occurred, for a moment, was annihilated; the heart went back with the rapid wing of Memory, to the hours of joy that were gone; and Leyton opened wide his arms, exclaiming, "Edith! Edith!"

She could not resist. She had no power to struggle. Love, stronger than herself, was master; and, starting up, she cast herself upon his bosom, and there wept.

"Dear, dear girl!" he said, "then you love me still,—then Digby's assurance is true—then you have not forgotten poor Harry Leyton—then his preserving hope, his long endurance, his unwavering love, his efforts, his success, have not been all in vain!—Dear, dear Edith! This hour repays me for all—for all. Dangers and adversities, and wounds, and anguish of body and of mind, and sleepless nights, and days of bitter thought—I would endure them all. All?—ay, tenfold all—for this one hour!" and he pressed her closer and closer to his heart.

"Nay, Harry—nay," cried Edith, still clinging to him; "but hear me, hear me—or if you speak such words of tenderness, you will break my heart, or drive me mad."

"Good heaven!" exclaimed Leyton, unclasping his arms, "what is it that you say? Edith—my Edith—my own, my vowed, my bride! But now, you seemed to share the joy you gave,—to love, as you are loved; and now——"

"I do love you—oh! I do love you!" cried Edith, vehemently; "add not a doubt of that to all I suffer. Ever, ever have I loved you, without change, without thought of change. But yet—but yet—. I may have fancied that you have forgotten me—I may have thought it strange that you did not write—that my letters remained unanswered; but still I loved, still I have been true to you."

"I did write, my Edith. I received no letters," said Leyton, sadly; "we have both been wronged, my dear girl. My letters were returned in a cover directed in your own hand: but that trick I understand—that I see through. Oh, do not let any one deceive you again, beloved girl! You have been my chief—I might say my *only* thought; for the memory of you has mingled with every other idea, and made the whole your own. In the camp and in the field, I have endured and fought for Edith; in the council and in the court, I have struggled and striven for her; she has been the end and object of every effort, the ruling power of my whole mind. And now, Edith—now your soldier has returned to you. He has won every step towards the crowning reward of his endeavours; he has risen to competence, to command, to some honour in the service of his country; and he can proudly say to her he loves, Cast from you the fortune for which men dared to think I sought you—come to your lover, come to your husband, as dowerless as he was when they parted us; and let all the world see and know, that it was your love, not your wealth, I coveted—this dear hand, that dear heart, not base gold, that I desired. Oh, Edith, in Heaven's name, cast me not now headlong down from the height of hope and joy to which you have raised me, for fear a heart and spirit, too long depressed, should never find strength to rise again."

Edith staggered back and sank down upon the sofa, covering her eyes, and only murmuring—"I do love you, Harry, beyond life itself.—Oh, that I were dead!—oh, that I were dead!"

There was a terrible struggle in Henry Leyton's bosom. He could not understand the agitation that he witnessed; had it borne anything like the character of joy, even of surprise, all would have been clear; but it was evidently very different. It was joy overborne by sorrow. It was evidently a struggle of love with some influence, perhaps not stronger, yet terrible in its effect. He was a man of quick decision and strong resolution—qualities not always combined; and he overcame himself in a moment. He saw that he was loved—still deeply, truly loved; and that was a great point. He saw that Edith was grieved to the soul—he saw that he himself could not feel more intensely the anguish she inflicted than she did, that she was wringing her own heart while she was wringing his, and felt a double pang; and that was a strong motive for calmness, if not for fortitude. Her last words, "I wish I were dead!" restored him fully to himself; and following her to the sofa, he seated himself beside her, gently took her hand in his, and pressed his lips upon it.

"Edith," he said—"my own dear Edith, let us be calm! Thank you, my beloved, for one moment of happiness, the first I have known for years; and now let us talk, as quietly as may be, of anything that may have arisen which should justly cause Henry Leyton's return to make Edith Croyland wish herself dead. Your uncle will not be long ere he arrives; I left him on the road; and it is by his full consent that I am here."

"Oh no, Harry—no!" said Edith, turning at first to his comment on her words, "it is not your return that makes me wish myself dead; but it is, that circumstances—dark and terrible circumstances—which were only made known to me an hour before your arrival, have turned all the joy, the pure, the almost unmixed joy, that

I should have felt at seeing you again, into a well of bitterness. It is that I cannot, that I dare not explain to you those circumstances—that you will think me wrong, unkind—fickle, perhaps,—perhaps even mad, in whatsoever way I may act."

"But surely you can say something, dear Edith," said her lover; "you can give some hint of the cause of all I see. You tell me in one breath that you love me still, yet wish you were dead; and show evidently that my coming has been painful to you."

"No, no, Harry," she answered, mournfully, "do not say so. Painful to me?—oh, no! It would be the purest joy that ever I yet knew, were it not that—But why did you not come earlier, Harry? Why, when your horse stood upon that hill, did you not turn his head hither? Would that you had, would that you had! My fate would have been already decided. Now it is all clouds and darkness. I knew you instantly. I could see no feature; I could but trace a figure on horseback, wrapped in a large cloak; but the instinct of love told me who it was. Oh! why did you not come then?"

"Because it would have been dishonest, Edith," answered Leyton, gravely. "Your uncle had been my father's friend, my uncle's friend. In a kindly manner he invited me here some time ago, as a perfect stranger, under the name of Captain Osborn. You were not here then; and I thought I could not in honour come under his roof, when I found you were here, without telling him who I really was. He appointed this day to meet me at Woodchurch at two; and I dared not venture, after all that has passed between your family and mine, to seek you in his dwelling, ere I had seen and explained myself to him. I knew you were here: I gazed up at these windows with a yearning of the heart that nearly overcame my resolution——"

"I saw you gaze, Harry," answered Edith; "and I say still, would that you had come.—Yet you were right.—It might have saved me much misery; but you were right. And now listen to the fate that is before me — to the choice I have to make, as far as I can explain it—and yet what words can I use?—But it must be done. I must not leave anything unperformed, that can prevent poor Edith Croyland from becoming an object of hatred and contempt in Henry Leyton's eyes. Little as I can do to defend myself, I must do it."

She paused, gazed up on high for a moment, and then laid her hand upon his.

"Henry, I do love you," she said. "Nay, more, I am yours, plighted to you by bonds I cannot and I dare not break—vows, I mean, the most solemn, as well as the ties of long affection. Yet, if I wed you, I am miserable for life. Self-reproach, eternal self-reproach—the most terrible of all things—to which no other mental or corporeal pain can ever reach, would prey upon my heart for ever, and bear me down into the grave. Peace—rest, I should have none. A voice would be for ever howling in my ear a name that would poison sleep, and make each waking moment an hour of agony. I can tell you no more on this side of the question; but so it is. It seems fated that I should bring misery one way or another upon him who is dearest to me."

"I cannot comprehend," exclaimed Leyton, in surprise. "Your father has heard, I suppose, that I am here, and has menaced you with his curse."

"Oh, no!" answered Edith; "far from it. He was here but now; he spoke of you, Henry, as you deserve. He told me how he had loved you and esteemed you in your young days; how, though angry at first at our rash engagement, he would have consented in the end; but—there was a fatal 'but,' Henry—an impediment not to be surmounted. I must not tell you what it is—I cannot, I dare not explain. But listen to what he said besides. You have heard one part of the choice; hear the other: it is to wed a man whom I abhor—despise—contemn—whose very look is fearful to me; to ask you to give me back the vows I plighted, in order—in order," and she spoke very low, "that I may sacrifice myself for my father, that I may linger out a few weeks of wretchedness, and then sink into the grave, which is now my only hope."

"And do you ask me, Edith?" inquired Leyton, in a sad and solemn tone—"do you, Edith Croyland, really and truly ask me to give you back those vows? Speak, beloved—speak; for my heart is well nigh bursting."

He paused, and she was silent; covering her eyes with her hands, while her bosom heaved, as if she were struggling for breath. "No, no, no, Harry!" she cried, at length, as if the effort were vain, "I cannot, I cannot! Oh, Harry, Harry! I wish that I were dead!" and, casting her arms round his neck, she wept upon his breast again.

Henry Leyton drew her closer to him with his left arm round her waist; but pressed his right hand on his brow, and gazed on vacancy. Both remained without speaking for a time; but at length he said, in a voice more calm than might have been expected, "Let us consider this matter, Edith. You have been terrified by some means; a tale has been told you, which has agitated and alarmed you, which has overcome your resolution, that now has endured more than six years, and doubtless that tale has been well devised.—Are you sure that it is true? —Forgive this doubt in regard to one who is near and dear to you; but when such deceits have been practised, as those which we know have been used to delude us, I must be suspicious.—Are you sure that it is true, I say?

"Too true, too true!" answered Edith, shaking her head, mournfully—"that tale explains all, too,—even those deceits you mention. No, no, it is but too true—it could not be feigned—besides, I remember so many things, all tending to the same. It is true—I cannot doubt it."

Sir Henry Leyton paused, and twice began to speak, but twice stopped, as if the words he was about to utter, cost him a terrible struggle to speak. At length he said, "And the man, Edith—the man they wish you to marry—who is he?"

"Ever the same," answered Edith, bending down her head, and her cheek, which had been as pale as death, glowing like crimson—"the same, Richard Radford."

"What! a felon!" exclaimed Leyton, turning round, with his brows bent; "a felon, after whom my soldiers and the officers of justice are now hunting through the country! Sir Robert Croyland must be mad! But I tell you, Edith, that man shall never stand within a church again, till it be the chapel of the gaol. Let him make his peace with Heaven; for if he be caught—and caught he shall be—there is no mercy for him on earth. But surely there must be some mistake. You cannot have understood your father rightly, or he cannot know——"

"Oh! yes, yes!" replied Edith; "he knows all; and it is the same. Ay, and within four days, too—that he may take me with him in his flight."

"Ere four days be over," answered her lover, sternly, "he shall no more think of bridals."

"And what will become of my father, then!" said Edith, gazing steadily down upon the ground. "It is I—I that shall have done it. Alas, alas! which way shall I turn?"

There was something more than sorrow in her countenance; there was anguish—almost agony; and Sir Henry Leyton was much moved. "Turn to me, Edith," he said; "turn to him who loves you better than life; and there is no sacrifice that he will not make for you, but his honour. Tell me, have you made any promise? —have you given your father your consent?"

"No," answered Edith, eagerly; "no, I have not. He took my words as consent, though ere they were half finished, the horror and pain of all I heard overcame me, and I fainted. But I did not consent, Harry—I could not consent, without your permission.—Oh, Harry, aid and support me!"

"Listen to me, my beloved," replied Leyton; "wealth, got by any means, is this man's object. I gather from what you say, that your father has some cause to dread him—give up to him this much-coveted fortune—let him take it—ay, and share Henry Leyton's little wealth. I desire nothing but yourself."

"Alas, Henry, it is all in vain!" answered Edith; I have offered it—I knew your noble, generous heart. I knew that wealth would make no difference to him I loved, and offered to resign everything. My father, even before he came hither, offered him my sister—offered to make her the sacrifice, as she is bound by no promises, and to give her an equal portion; but it was all refused."

"Then there is some other object," said her lover; "some object that may, perhaps, tend even to more misery than you dream of, Edith. Believe me, my beloved—oh! believe me, did I but see how I could deliver you—were I sure that any act of mine would give you peace, no sacrifice on my part would seem too great. At present, however, I see nothing clearly—all is darkness and shadow around. I know not, that if I give you back your promise, and free you from your vow, that I shall not be contributing to make you wretched. How, then, am I to act? You are sure, dear one, that you have not consented?"

"Quite sure," answered Edith; "and it so happened, that there was one who heard my words as well as my father. He, indeed, took them as consent, and hurried away to Mr. Radford, without giving me time to recover and say more. Read that, Harry," and she put the note her father had left into his hands.

"It is fortunate you were heard by another," replied Leyton. "Hark! there is your uncle's carriage coming.—Four days, did he say—four days? Well, then, dear Edith, will you trust in me? Will you leave your fate in the hands of one who will do anything on earth for your happiness?—and will you never doubt, though you may be kept in suspense, that I will so act as to deliver you, if I can, without bringing ruin on your father."

"It is worse than ruin," answered Edith, with the tears rolling down her cheeks—"it is death. But I will trust to you, Henry—I will trust implicitly. But tell me how to act—tell me what I am to do."

"Leave this matter as it is," answered her lover, hearing Mr. Croyland's carriage stop at the door;—"your father has snatched too eagerly at your words. Perhaps he has done so to gain time; but, at all events, the fault is his, not yours. If he speaks to you on the subject, you must tell the truth, and say you did not consent; but in everything else be passive—let him do with you what he will—take you to the altar, if he so pleases; but there must be the final struggle, Edith. There you must boldly and aloud refuse to wed a man you cannot love. There let the memory of your vows to me be ever present with you. It may seem cruel; but I exact it for your own sake. In the meantime, take means to let me know everything that happens, be it small or great—cast off all reserve towards Digby; tell him all, everything that takes place; tell your sister, too, or any one who can bear me the tidings. I shall be nearer than you think."

"Oh, Heaven, how will this end!" cried Edith, putting her hand in his—"God help me, Harry—God help me!"

"He will, dear girl," answered Leyton—"I feel sure he will. But remember what I have said. Fail not to tell Digby, or Zara, or any one who can bear the tidings to me, everything that occurs, every word that is spoken, every step that is taken. Think nothing too trifling.

But there is your uncle's voice in the passage. Can you not inform him of that which you think yourself bound not to tell me? I mean the particulars of your father's situation."

"No; oh no!" replied Edith—"I dare tell no one, especially not my uncle. Though kind, and generous, and benevolent, yet he is hasty, and he might ruin all. Dared I tell any one on earth, Henry, it would be you; and if I loved you before—oh, how I must love you now, when instead of the anger, or even heat, which I expected you to display, you have shown yourself ready to sacrifice all for one who is hardly worthy of you."

Leyton pressed her to his bosom, and replied, "Real love is unselfish, Edith. I tell you, dearest, that I die if I lose you; yet, Edith Croyland shall never do what is wrong for Henry Leyton's sake. If in the past we did commit an error, if I should not have engaged you by vows without your parent's consent—though God knows that error has been bitterly visited on my head!—I am still ready to make atonement to the best of my power; but I will not consent that you should be causelessly made miserable, or sacrifice yourself and me, without benefit to any one. Trust to me, Edith—trust to me."

"I will, I will!" answered Edith Croyland; "who can I trust to else?"

Mr. Croyland was considerate; and knowing that Sir Henry Leyton was with his niece—for his young friend had passed him on the road—he paused for a moment in the vestibule, giving various orders and directions, in order to afford them a few minutes more of private conversation. When he went in, he was surprised to find Edith's face full of deep grief, and her eyes wet with tears, and still more when Leyton, after kissing her fair cheek, advanced towards him, saying, "I must go, my dear friend, nor can I accept your kind invitation to stay here to-night. But I am about to show myself a bold man, and ask you to give me almost the privilege of a son—that is, of coming and going, for the four or five next days, at my own will, and without question."

"What's all this?—what's all this?" cried Mr. Croyland; "a lovers' quarrel?—Ha, Edith? Ha, Harry?"

"Oh, no," answered Edith, giving her uncle her hand; "there never can be a quarrel between me and Henry Leyton."

"Well, then, what is it all?" exclaimed Mr. Croyland, turning from one to the other. "Mystery—mystery! I hate mystery, Harry Leyton.—However, you shall have your privilege; the doors shall be open. Come—go—do what you like. But if you are not a great fool, you will order over a post-chaise and four this very night, put her in, and be off for Gretna Green. I'll give you my parental benediction."

"I am afraid, my dear sir," answered Leyton, "that cannot be. Edith has told me various things since I saw her, which require to be dealt with in a different way. I trust, that in whatever I do, my conduct will be such as to give you satisfaction; and whether the result be fortunate or otherwise, I shall never, till the last hour of life, forget the kindness you have shown me. And now, my dear sir, adieu for the present, for I have much to do this night."

Thus saying, he shook the old gentleman's hand, and departed with a heavy heart and anxious mind. During his onward ride, his heart did not become lighter; his mind was only more burdened with cares. As long as he was in Edith's presence, he had borne up and struggled against all that he felt; for he saw that she was already overwhelmed with grief, and he feared to add to it; but now his thoughts were all confusion. With incomplete information—in circumstances the most difficult—anxious to save her he loved, even at any sacrifice on his own part, yet seeing no distinct means of acting in any direction without danger to her—he looked around him in vain for any resource; or, if he formed a plan one moment, he rejected it the next. He knew Edith's perfect truth, he knew the quiet firmness and power of her mind too well to doubt one tittle of that which she had stated; and though at first sight he thought the proofs he possessed of Mr. Radford's participation in the late smuggling transaction were quite sufficient to justify that person's immediate arrest, and proposed that it should take place immediately, yet the next moment he recollected what might be the result to Sir Robert Croyland, and hesitated how to act. Then, again, he turned his eyes to the circumstances in which Edith's father was placed, and asked himself, what could be the mystery which so terribly overshadowed him? Edith had said that his life was at stake; and Leyton tortured his imagination in vain to find some explanation of such a fact.

"Can he have been deceiving her?" he asked himself more than once. But then, again, he answered, "No, it must be true! He can have no ordinary motive in urging her to such a step; his whole character, his whole views are against it. Haughty and ostentatious, there must be some overpowering cause to make him seek to wed his daughter to a low ruffian—the son of an upstart, who owed his former wealth to fraud, and who is now, if all tales be true, nearly bankrupt,—to wed Edith, a being of grace, of beauty, and of excellence, to a villain like this—a felon and a fugitive—and to send her forth into the wide world, to share the wanderings of a man she hates! The love of life must be a strange thing in some men. One would have thought that a thousand lives were nothing to such a sacrifice. Yet, the tale must be true; this old man must have Sir Robert's life in his power. But how—how? that is the question. Perhaps Digby can discover something. At all events, I must see him without delay."

In such thoughts, Sir Henry Leyton rode on fast to Woodchurch, accomplishing in twenty minutes that which took good Mr. Croyland, with his pampered horses, more than an hour to perform; and springing from his charger at the door of the inn, he was preparing to go up and write to Sir Edward Digby, when Captain Irby, on the one hand, and his own servant on the other, applied for attention.

"Mr. Warde is up stairs, sir," said the servant; "he has been waiting about half an hour."

But Leyton turned to the officer, asking, "What is it, Captain Irby?"

"Two or three of the men, sir, who have

been taken," replied Captain Irby, "have expressed a wish to make a statement. One of them is badly wounded, too; but I did not know how to act till you arrived, as we had no magistrate here."

"Was it quite voluntary?" demanded the young officer; "no inducements held out—no questions asked?"

"Quite voluntary, sir," answered the other. "They sent to ask for you; and when I went, in your absence, they told me what it was they desired; but I refused to take the deposition till you arrived, for fear of getting myself into a scrape."

"It must be taken," replied the colonel. "Of whatever value it may be judged hereafter, we must not refuse it when offered. I will come to them in a moment, Irby;" and entering the house, but without going up stairs, he wrote a few lines, in the bar, to Sir Edward Digby, requesting to see him without delay. Then, calling his servant, he said, "Tell Mr. Warde I will be with him in a few minutes; after which, mount yourself, and carry this note over to Harbourne House, to Sir Edward Digby. Give it into his own hand; but remember, it is my wish that you should not mention my name there at all. Do you know the place?"

"Yes, sir," replied the man; and, leaving him to fulfil his errand, the colonel returned to the door of the house, to accompany Captain Irby.

CHAPTER II.

We must now return for a time to Harbourne House, where, after Sir Robert Croyland's departure, his guest had endeavoured in vain, during the whole morning, to obtain a few minutes' private conversation with the baronet's youngest daughter. Now, it was not in the least degree, that Mrs. Barbara's notions of propriety interfered to prevent the two young people from being alone together; for, on the contrary, Mrs. Barbara was a very lenient and gentle-minded person, and thought it quite right that any two human beings who were likely to fall in love with each other, should have every opportunity of doing so, to their hearts' content. But it so happened, from a sort of fatality which hung over all her plans, that whenever she interfered with anything,—which, indeed, she always did, with everything she could lay her hands upon, —the result was sure to be directly the contrary to that which she intended. It might be, indeed, that she did not always manage matters quite judiciously, that she acted without considering all the circumstances of the case; and undoubtedly it would have been quite as well if she had not acted at all when she was not asked.

In the present instance, when she had remained in the drawing-room with her niece and Sir Edward, for near half an hour after her brother had departed, it just struck her that they might wish to be alone together; for she had made up her mind by this time, that the young officer's visit was to end in a love affair; and, as the very best means of accomplishing the desired object, instead of going to speak with the housekeeper, or to give orders to the dairy-maid, or to talk to the steward, —as any other prudent, respectable, and well-arranged aunt would have done—she said to her niece, as if a sudden thought had occurred to her, "I don't think Sir Edward Digby has ever seen the library. Zara, my dear, you had better show it to him. There are some very curious books there, and the manuscript in vellum, with all the kings' heads painted."

Zara felt that it was rather a coarse piece of work which her aunt had just turned out of hand; and being a little too much susceptible of ridicule, she did not like to have anything to do with it, although, to say the truth, she was very anxious herself for the few minutes that Mrs. Barbara was inclined to give her.

"Oh, I dare say, my dear aunt," she replied, "Sir Edward Digby does not care anything about old books!—I don't believe they have been opened for these fifty years."

"The greater the treasure, Miss Croyland," answered the young officer; "I can assure you nothing delights me more than an old library; so I think I shall go and find it out myself, if you are not disposed to show it to me."

Zara Croyland remembered, with a smile, that Sir Edward Digby had met with no great difficulty in finding it out for himself on a previous occasion. She rose, however, with her colour a little heightened; for his invitation was a very palpable one, and she did not know what conclusions her aunt might be pleased to draw, or to insinuate to others; and, leading the way towards the library, she opened the door, expecting to find the room untenanted. There, however, before her eyes, standing opposite to a book-case, with a large folio volume of divinity in his hand, stood the clergyman of the parish; and he instantly turned round his head, with spectacles on nose, and advanced to pay his respects to Miss Croyland and Sir Edward Digby. Now, the clergyman was a very worthy man; but he had one of those peculiarities, which, if peculiarities were systematically classed, would be referred to the bore genus. He was frequently unaware of when people had had enough of him; and consequently on the present occasion—after he had informed Zara, that finding that her father was out, he had taken the liberty of walking into the library to look at a book he wanted—he put back that book, and attacked Sir Edward Digby, totis viribus, upon the state of the weather, the state of the country, and the state of the smugglers. The later topic, as it was the predominant one in every man's mind at that moment, and in that part of the country, occupied him rather longer than a sermon, though his parishioners occasionally thought his sermons quite sufficiently extensive for any sleep-resisting powers of the human frame to withstand; and then, when Sir Edward and Zara, forgetting, in the interest which they seemed to take in his discourse, that they had come into the library to look at the books, walked out upon the terrace, he walked out with them; and as they turned up and down, he turned up and down also, for full an hour.

Zara could almost have cried in the end; but, as out of the basest refuse of our stable-yards, grow the finest flowers of our gardens, so good is ever springing up from evil; and in the end the worthy clergyman gave his two companions the first distinct account which they had received of the dispersion of Mr. Radford's band of smugglers, and of the eager pursuit of young Radford which was taking place throughout the country.

Thus passed the morning, with one event or other of little consequence, presenting obstacles to any free communication between two people, who were almost as desirous of some private conversation as if they had been lovers.

A little before three o'clock, however, Zara Croyland who had been looking out of the window, suddenly quitted the drawing-room; and Sir Edward Digby, who maintained his post, was left to entertain Mrs. Barbara, which he did to the best of his abilities. He was still in full career, a little enjoying, to say sooth, some of the good lady's minor absurdities, when Zara re-entered the room with a quick step, and a somewhat eager look. Her fair cheek was flushed too; and her face had in it that sort of determined expression which often betrays that there has been a struggle in the mind, as to some step about to be taken, and that victory has not been achieved without an effort.

"Sir Edward Digby," she said, in a clear and distinct tone, "I want to speak with you for a few moments, if you please."

Mrs. Barbara looked shocked, and internally

wondered that Zara could not have made some little excuse for engaging Sir Edward in private conversation.

"She might have asked him to go and see a flower, or offered to play him a tune on the harpsichord, or taken him to look at the dove-cot, or anything," thought Mrs. Barbara.

The young officer, however, instantly started up, and accompanied his fair inviter towards the library, to which she led the way with a hurried and eager step.

"Let us come in here!" she said, opening the door; but the moment she was within, she sank into a chair and clasped her hands together.

Sir Edward Digby shut the door, and then advanced towards her, a good deal surprised and somewhat alarmed by the agitation he saw her display. She did not speak for a moment, as if completely overpowered, and feeling for her more deeply than he himself knew, her companion took her hand and tried to soothe her, saying, "Be calm—be calm, my dear Miss Croyland! You know you can trust in me, and if I can aid you in any way, command me."

"I know not what to do, or what to say," cried Zara; "but I am sure, Sir Edward, you will find excuses for me; and therefore I will make none—though I may perhaps seem somewhat bold in dealing thus with one whom I have only known a few days."

"There are circumstances which sometimes make a few days equal to many years," replied Sir Edward Digby. "It is so, my dear young lady, with you and I. Therefore, without fear or hesitation, tell me what it is that agitates you, and how I can serve you. I am not fond of making professions; but if it be in human power, it shall be done."

"I know not, whether it can be done or not," said Zara; "but if not, there is nothing but ruin and desolation for two people, whom we both love. You saw my father set out this morning. Did you remark the course he took? It was over to my uncle's, for I watched him from the window. He passed back again some time ago, but then struck off towards Mr. Radford's. All that made me uneasy; but just now, I saw Edith's maid coming up towards the house; and eager for tidings, I hurried away.—Good Heavens, what tidings she has borne me!"

"They must be evil ones, I see," answered Digby; "but I trust not such as to preclude all chance of remedying what may have gone wrong. When two or three people act together zealously, dear lady, there are very few things they cannot accomplish."

"Yes, but how to explain!" exclaimed Zara; "yet I must be short; for otherwise my aunt will be in upon us. Now, Sir Edward Digby," she continued, after thinking for a moment, "I know you are a man of honour—I am sure you are; and I ask you to pledge me that honour, that you will never reveal to any one what I am going to tell you; for I know not whether I am about to do right or wrong—whether, in trying to save one, I may not be bringing down ruin upon others. Do you give me your honour?"

"Most assuredly!" answered her companion. "I will never repeat a word that you say, unless with your permission, on my honour!"

"Well, then," replied Zara, in a faint voice,

"Mr. Radford has my father's life in hi: power. How, I know not—how, I cannot tell But so it is; and such are the tidings that Caro line has just brought us. Mr. Radford's con ference with him this morning was not fo: nothing. Immediately after, he went over t(Edith; he told her some tale which the girl di(not distinctly hear; but, it seems, some pape: which Mr. Radford possesses was spoken of, an(the sum of the whole matter was, that my poor sweet sister was told, if she did not consent, withi: four days, to marry that hateful young man, sh(would sacrifice her father's life. He left he: fainting, and has ridden over to bear her con sent to Mr. Radford."

"But, did she consent?" exclaimed Si: Edward Digby, in surprise and consternation— "Did she really yield?"

"No—no!" answered Zara, "she did not The girl said she heard her words, and the; were not in truth a consent. But my father chos(to take them as such, and left her even befor(she recovered."

I have already shown the effect of the sam(

account upon Sir Henry Leyton, with all the questions which it suggested to his mind; and the impression produced upon his friend, as a man of sense and a man of the world, were so similar, that it may be needless to give any detailed statement of his first observations or inquiries. Zara soon satisfied him, however, that the tale her father had told, was not a mere device to frighten Edith into a compliance with his wishes; and then came the question, What was to be done?

"It is, in truth, a most painful situation in which your sister is placed," said Digby, after some consideration; "but think you that this man, this Radford, cannot be bought off? Money must be to him—if he be as totally ruined as people say—the first consideration; and I know Leyton so well, that I can venture to promise nothing of that kind shall stand in the way, if we can but free your sister from the terrible choice put before her."

Zara shook her head sadly, saying, "No; that hope is vain!—The girl tells me," she added, with a faint smile, which was quickly succeeded by a blush, "that she heard my father say he had offered me—poor me! to Richard Radford, with the same fortune as Edith, but had been refused."

"And would you have consented?" demanded Sir Edward Digby, in a more eager tone than he had yet used.

"Nay," replied Zara, "that has nought to do with the present question. Suffice it, that this proves that gold is not his only object."

"Nay, but answer me," persevered her companion; "would you have consented? It may have much to do with the question yet." He fixed his eyes gravely upon her face, and took the fair, small hand, that lay upon the arm of the chair, in his.—It was something very like making love, and Zara felt a strange sensation at her heart; but she turned away her face, and answered, with a very pale cheek, "I would die for my father, Sir Edward; but I could not wed Richard Radford."

Sir Edward raised her hand to his lips, and pressed them on it. "I thought so!" he said—"I thought so! And now, heart, and mind and hand, and spirit, to save your sister, Zara! I have hunted many a fox in my day, and I don't think the old one of Radford Hall will escape me. The greatest difficulty is, not to compromise your father in any way; but that shall be cared for, too, to the very best of my power, be assured. Henceforth, dear lady, away with all reserve between us. While I am in this house, it will be absolutely necessary for you to communicate with me freely, and probably very often. Have no hesitation; have no scruple as to hour, or manner, or means. Trust to my honour as you have trusted this day; and you shall never find it fail you. I will enter into such explanations with my servant, Somers, in regard to poor Leyton, as will make him think it nothing strange, if you send him for me at any time. He is as discreet as a privy councillor; and you must, therefore, have no hesitation."

"I will not," answered Zara; "for I would do anything to save my sister from such a fate; and I do believe you will not think—you will not imagine——"

She paused in some confusion; and Sir Ed ward Digby answered, with a smile—but kindly and a gentlemanly one, "Let m imagination do as it will, Zara. Depend upo it, it shall do you no wrong; and believe m when I say, that I can hardly feel so much pai at these circumstances as I otherwise might since they bring me into such near and frequen communication with you."

"Hush, hush!" she answered, somewha gravely; "I can think of nothing now but m poor sister; and you must not, Sir Edward, b one compliment, or fine speech—nay, nor by on kind speech either," she added, laying her han upon his arm, and looking up in his face, with glowing cheek—"for I know you mean it as kin —you must not, indeed, throw any embarrass ment over an intercourse, which is necessary a present, and which is my only hope and resource in the circumstances in which we are placed So now tell me what you are going to do; fo you seemed, but now, as if you were about t set out somewhere."

"I am going to Woodchurch instantly," replied Digby. "Sir Henry Leyton must be there still——"

"Sir Henry Leyton!" exclaimed Zara; "then he has, indeed, been a successful campaigner."

"Most successful, and most deservedly so," answered his friend. "No man but Wolfe won more renown; and if he can but gain this battle, Leyton will have all that he desires on earth. But I will not stay here, skirmishing on the flanks, dear lady, while the main body is engaged. I will ride over as fast as possible, see Leyton, consult with him, and be back, if possible, by dinner time. If not, you must tell your father not to wait for me, as I was suddenly called away on business."

"But how shall I know the result of your expedition?" demanded Zara; "we shall be surrounded, I fear, by watchful eyes."

"We must trust to fortune and our own efforts to afford us some means of communication," replied Digby. "But remember, dearest lady, that for this great object, you have promised to cast away all reserve. For the time, at least you must look upon Edward Digby as a brother and treat him as such."

"That I will!" answered the fair girl, heartily; and Digby, leaving her to explain their conduct to her aunt as she best might, ordered his horse and rode away towards Woodchurch, in haste

Pulling in his rein at the door of the little inn, he inquired which was Sir Henry Leyton's room, and was directed up stairs; but on opening the door of the chamber which had been pointed out, he found no one in it, but the somewhat strange-looking old man, whom we have once before seen with Leyton, at Hythe.

"Ah, Mr. Warde, you here!" exclaimed Sir Edward Digby. "Leyton told me you were in England. But where is he? I have business of some importance to talk with him upon;" and as he spoke, he shook the old man's hand warmly.

"I know you have," answered Mr. Warde gazing upon him—"at least, I can guess that such is the case.—So have I; and doubtless the subject is the same."

"Nay, I should think not," replied Digby; "mine refers only to private affairs."

The old man smiled; and that sharp-featured, rude countenance assumed an expression of indescribable sweetness: "Mine is the same," he said. "You come to speak of Edith Croyland—so do I."

"Indeed!" cried his companion, a good deal surprised; "you are a strange being, Mr. Warde. You seem to learn men's secrets, whether they will or not."

"There is nothing strange on earth, but man's blindness," answered the other; "everything is so simple, when once explained, that its simplicity remains the only marvel.—But here he comes. Let me converse with him first. Then, when he is aware of all that I know, you shall have my absence, or my presence, as it suits you."

While he was speaking, the voice of Henry Leyton was heard below, and then his step upon the stairs; and, before Digby could answer, he was in the room. His face was grave, but not so cloudy as it had been when he returned to

Woodchurch, half-an-hour before. He welcomed Mr. Warde frankly, and cordially; but turned immediately to Sir Edward Digby, saying, "You have been quick indeed, Digby. I could not have conceived that my letter had reached you."

"I got no letter," answered Digby; "perhaps it missed me on the way; for, the corn being down, I came straight across the country."

"It matters not—it matters not," answered Leyton; "so you are here—that is enough. I have much to say to you, and that of immediate importance."

"I know it already," answered Digby. "But here is our good friend, Warde, who seems to have something to say to you on the same subject."

Sir Henry Leyton turned towards the old man with some surprise. "I think Digby must be mistaken," he said, "for though, I am aware, from what you told me some little time ago, that you have been in this part of the country before, yet it must have been long ago, and you can know nothing of the events which have affected myself since."

The old man smiled, and shook his head. "I know more than you imagine," he answered. "It is, indeed, long since first I was in this land; but not so long since I was here last; and all its people and its things, its woods, its villages, its hills, are as familiar to me—ay, more so than to you. Of yourself, Leyton, and your fate, I also know much—I might say I know all; for certainly I know more than you do, can do more than you are able to do, will do more than you can. To show you what I know; I will give you a brief summary of your own history—at least, that part of it, of which you think I know nothing. Young, eager, and impatient, you were thrown constantly into the society of one, good, beautiful, gentle, and true. You had much encouragement from those who should not have given it, unless they had the intention of continuing it to the end. You loved, and were beloved; and then, in the impatience of your boyish ardour, you bound Edith Croyland to yourself, without her parent's knowledge and consent, by vows which, whatever human laws may say, are indissoluble by

the law of Heaven; and therein you did wron
It was a great error.—Do I say right?"

"It was, indeed," answered Sir Henry Le
ton, casting down his eyes sternly on the grou
—"it was, indeed."

"More—I will tell you more," continued M
Warde; "you have bitterly repented it, and bi
terly suffered for it. You are suffering even now

"Not for it," replied the young officer-
"not for it. My sufferings are not consequenc
of my fault."

"You are wrong," answered the old man
"wrong, as you will find. But I will go on, an
tell you what you have done this day. Tho
who have behaved ill to you have been punishe
likewise; and their punishment is working itse
out, but sweeping you in within its vortex. Yo
have been over to see Edith Croyland. She h
told you her tale. You have met in love, an
parted in sorrow.—Is it not so? And now yo
know not which way to turn for deliverance."

"It is so, indeed, my good friend," sai
Leyton, sadly; "but how you have discovere
all this, I cannot divine."

"That has nought to do with the subject," answered Warde. "Now tell me, Leyton, tell me—and remember you are dearer to me than you know—are you prepared to make atonement for your fault? The only atonement in your power—to give back to Edith the vows she plighted, to leave her free to act as she may judge best. I have marked you well, as you know, for years. I have seen you tried as few men, perhaps, are tried; and you have come out pure and honest. The last trial is now arrived; and I ask you here, before your friend, your worldly friend, if you are ready to act honestly still, and to annul engagements that you had no right to contract?"

"I am," answered Sir Henry Leyton; "I am, if ——"

"Ay, if! There is ever an 'if' when men would serve their own purposes against their conscience," said Mr. Warde, sternly.

"Nay, but hear me, my good friend," replied the young officer. "I have every respect for you. Your whole character commands it and deserves it, as wel as your profession; but, at the same time, though I may think fit to answer yo candidly, in matters where I would reject ar other man's interference, yet I must shape n answer as I think proper, and rule my condu according to my own views. You must, ther fore, hear me out. I say that I am ready give back to Edith Croyland the vows sl plighted me, to set her free from all engag ments, to leave her, as far as possible, as if sl had never known Henry Leyton, whatever par it may cost me—*if* it can be proved to me th by so doing I have not given her up to miser as well as myself. My own wretchedness I ca bear—I have borne it long, cheered by oı little ray of hope. I can bear it still, eve though that light go out; but to know that l any act of mine—however seemingly generou or, as you term it, honest—I had yielded her ı to a life of anguish, that I could not bear. Sho me that this will not be the case; and, as I ha said before, I am ready to make the sacrifice, it cost me life. Nay, more: I returned hith prepared, if at the last, and with every effort avert it, I found that circumstances of which know not the extent, rendered the keeping of her vows to me more terrible in its consequences than her union with another, however hateful he may be,—I came hither prepared, I say, in such a case, to set her free; and I will do it!"

The old man took both his hands, and gazed on him with a look of glad satisfaction. "Honest to the last," he said—"honest to the last! The resolution to do this, is as good as the deed; for I know you are not one to fail where you have resolved.—But those who might exact the sacrifice are not worthy of it. Your willingness has made the atonement, Leyton; and I will deliver you from your difficulty."

"You, Mr. Warde!" exclaimed Sir Edward Digby; "I cannot suppose that you really have the power; or, perhaps, after all, you do not know the whole circumstances."

"Hush, hush, young man!" answered Warde, with a wave of the hand; "I know all, I see all, where you know little or nothing. You are a good youth, as the world goes—better than most of your bad class and station; but these matters are above you. Listen to me, Leyton.

Did not Edith tell you that her father had worked upon her, by fears for his safety—for his honour—for his life, perhaps?"

"Yes, indeed," exclaimed Leyton, eagerly, and with a ray of hope beginning to break upon him. "Was the tale not true, then?"

"I guessed so," answered the old man. "I was sure that would be the course at last. Nevertheless, the tale he told was true—too true. It was forced from him by circumstances. Yet, I have said I will deliver you from your difficulty; and I will. Pursue your own course; as you have commenced, go on to the end. I ask you not now to give Edith back her promises. Nay, I tell you, that her misery, her wretchedness—ay, tenfold more than any you could suffer—would be the consequence, if you did so. Let her go on firmly in her truth to the last; but tell her, that deliverance will come. Now I leave you; but, be under no doubt. Your course is clear; do all you can by your own efforts to save her; but it is I who must deliver her in the end."

Without any further farewell, he turned and

left the room; and Sir Henry Leyton and his friend remained for a minute or two in thought.

"His parting advice is the best," said Digby, at length; "and doubtless you will follow it, Leyton; but, of course, you will not trust so far to the word of a madman, as to neglect any means that may present themselves."

"He is not mad," answered Leyton, shaking his head. "When first he joined us in Canada, before the battle of Quebec, I thought as you do; but he is not mad, Digby. There are various shades of reason; and there may be a slight aberration in his mind from the common course of ordinary thought. He may be wrong in his reasonings, rash in his opinions, somewhat over-excited in imagination; but that is not madness. His promises give me hope, I will confess; but still I will act as if they had not been made. Now let us speak of our plans; and first tell me what has taken place at Harbourne; for you seem to know all the particulars already, which I sent for you to communicate, though how you learned them I cannot divine."

"Oh, my dear Leyton, if I were to tell you

all that has happened," replied Sir Edward Digby, "I should have to go on as long as a Presbyterian minister, or a popular orator. I had better keep to the point;" and he proceeded to relate to his friend the substance of the conversation which had last taken place between himself and Zara.

"It is most fortunate," answered Leyton, "that dear girl has thus become acquainted with the facts; for Edith would not have told her, and now we have some chance of obtaining information of all that occurs, which must be our great security. However—since I returned, I have obtained valuable information, which puts good Mr. Radford's liberty, if not his life, in my power. Three of the men whom we have taken, distinctly state that he sent them upon this expedition himself—armed, and mounted them; and therefore he is a party to the whole transaction. I have sent off a messenger to Mowle, the officer—as faithful and as true a fellow as ever lived—begging him to bring me up, without a moment's delay, a magistrate in whom he can trust; for one of the men is at the point of death, and all the justices round this place are so imbued with the spirit of smuggling, that I do not choose the depositions to be taken by them. I have received and written down the statements made, before witnesses; and the men have signed them; but I have no power in this case to administer an oath. As soon as the matter is in more formal train, I shall insist upon the apprehension of Mr. Radford, whatever be the consequences to Sir Robert Croyland; for here my duty to the country is concerned, and the very powers with which I am entrusted, render it imperative upon me so to act."

"If you can catch him—if you can catch him!" replied Sir Edward Digby. "But be sure, my dear Leyton, if he once discovers that you have got such a hold upon him, he will take care to render that matter difficult. You may find it troublesome, also, to get a magistrate to act as you desire; for they are all of the same leaven; and I fancy you have no power to do anything yourself except in aid and support of the civil authorities. You must be very careful, too, not to exceed your commission, where people might suspect that personal feelings are concerned."

"Personal feelings shall not bias me, Digby, even in the slightest degree," replied his friend. "I will act towards Mr. Radford, exactly as I would towards any other man who had committed this offence; and, as to the imputation of motives, I can well afford to treat such things with contempt. Were I, indeed, to act as I wish, I should not pursue this charge against the chief offender, in order not to bring down his vengeance suddenly upon Sir Robert Croyland's head, or should use the knowledge I possess merely to impose silence upon him through fear. But my duty is plain and straightforward; and it must be done. As to my powers, they are more extensive than you suppose. Indeed, I would have sooner thrown up my commission, than have undertaken a service I disliked, without sufficient authority to execute it properly. Thus, if no magistrate could be found to act as I might require, I would not scruple, with the aid of any officer of Customs, or even without, to apprehend this man on my own responsibility. But I think we shall easily find one who will do his duty."

"At all events," replied Sir Edward Digby, "you had better be cautious, my dear Leyton. If you are not too quick in your movements, you may perhaps trap the old bird and the young one together; and that will be a better day's sport than if you only got a single shot."

"Heaven send it may be before these fatal four days are over!" answered Leyton; "for then the matter will be decided and Edith delivered."

"Why, if you were to catch the young one, it would be sufficient for that object," said his friend.

But Leyton shook his head. "I fear not," he replied; "yet that purpose must not be neglected. Where he has concealed himself I cannot divine. It would seem certain that he never got out of Harbourne Wood, unless, indeed, it was by some of the bye-paths; and in that case, he surely must have been seen. I will have it searched, to-morrow, from end to end."

In the same strain the conversation proceeded for half-an-hour more, without any feasible plan of action having been decided upon, and with no further result than the arrangement of means for frequent and private communication. It was settled, indeed, that Leyton should fix his head-quarters at Woodchurch, and that two or three of the dragoons should be billeted at a small public-house on the road to Harbourne. To them any communication from Sir Edward Digby was to be conveyed by his servant, Somers, for the purpose of being forwarded to Woodchurch. Such matters being thus arranged, as far as circumstances admitted, the two friends parted; and Digby rode back to Harbourne House, which he reached, as may be supposed, somewhat later than Sir Robert Croyland's dinner-hour.

CHAPTER III.

About six o'clock on the evening of the same day, the cottage of Mrs. Clare was empty. The good widow herself stood at the garden gate, and looked up the road into the wood, along which the western sun was streaming low. After gazing for a moment in that direction, she turned her eyes to the left, and then down the edge of the wood, which stretched along in a tolerably even line till it reached the farther angle. The persevering dragoons were patrolling round it still; and Mrs. Clare murmured to herself, "How will he ever get out, if they keep such a watch?"

She was then going into the cottage again, when a hurried step caught her ear, coming apparently from the path which led from the side of Halden to the back of the house, and thence round the little garden into the road.

"That sounds like Harding's step," thought the widow; and her ear had not deceived her. In another minute, she beheld him turn the corner of the fence and come towards her; but there was a heated and angry look upon his face, which she had never seen there before; and—although she had acted for the best, and not without much consideration, in sending Kate upon Mr. Radford's commission, and not going herself—she feared that her daughter's lover might not be well pleased his bride should undertake such a task. As he came near, the symptoms of anger were more apparent still. There was the cloudy brow, the flashing eye, the hurried and impetuous walk, which she had often seen in her own husband—a man very similar in character to him who now approached her—when irritated by harsh words; and Widow Clare prepared to do all she could to soothe him ere Kate's return.

But Harding did not mention her he loved, demanding, while yet at some distance, "Where is Mr. Radford, Mrs. Clare?"

"He is not here, Mr. Harding," replied the widow; "he has not been here since the morning. But what makes you look so cross, Harding? You seem angry."

"And well I may be," answered Harding, with an oath. "What do you think they have set about?—That I informed against them, and betrayed them into the hands of the dragoons: when, they know, I saw them safe out of the Marsh; and it must have been their own stupidity, or the old man's babbling fears, that ruined them—always trusting people that were sure to be treacherous, and doubting those he knew to be honest. But I'll make him eat his words, or cram them down his throat with my fist."

"Why, he spoke quite kindly of you this morning, Harding," said the widow; "there must be some mistake."

"Mistake!" cried the smuggler, sharply; "there is no mistake.—It is all over Hythe and Folkestone already; and every one says that it came from him. Can you not tell me where he is gone?—Which way did he turn?"

"Towards his own house," replied Mrs. Clare; "but you had better come in, Harding, and get yourself cool before you go to him. You will speak angrily now, and mischief may come of it. I am sure there is some mistake."

"I will not sit down till I have made hi
own it," answered the smuggler. "Perhap
he is up at Harbourne. I'll go there. Whe
is Kate, Mrs. Clare?"

"She has gone towards Harbourne House
said the widow, not choosing, in the excite
state of his feelings, to tell him her daughter
errand; "but she will be back in one minut
if you will but come in."

"No," he replied; "I will come back by-an
by. Perhaps I shall meet her as I go;" and h
was turning towards the wood, when suddenl
at the spot where the road entered amongst th
trees, the pretty figure of Kate Clare, as trin
and neat, and simple as a wild flower, appeare
walking slowly back towards the cottage. B
she was not alone. By her side was a tal
handsome young man, dressed in full militar
costume, with his heavy sword under his arm
and a star upon his breast. He was bendin
down, talking to his fair companion with
friendly air, and she was answering him with
gay smile.

A pang shot through Harding's bosom: th
first that ever the poor girl had caused; no
indeed, would he have felt it then, had he no
been irritated; for his was a frank and confidin

.eart, open as the day, in which that foul and angerous guest, Suspicion, usually could find o lurking place. At first he did not recognise, a the glittering personage before his eyes, the rave, plain-looking stranger, who, a week or wo before, had conversed with him for a few ninutes on the cliffs near Sandgate; but he saw, s the two came on, that Kate raised her eyes; nd as soon as she perceived him standing by her nother, a look of joy lighted up her face, which nade him murmur to himself, "I'm a fool!"

The stranger, too, saw him; but it made no change in his demeanour; and the next noment, to Harding's surprise, the officer came orward somewhat more quickly, and took Widow Clare by the hand, saying, with a grave smile, "Do you not know me, Mrs. Clare?"

"Gracious Heaven!" cried the widow, drawing back and gazing at him, "Can it be you, sir?"

"Yes, indeed!" he answered. "Why, Kate here knew me directly, though she was but ten or eleven, I think, when I went away."

"Oh, that was because you were always so fond of her, Mr. Henry," replied Widow Clare. "Gracious! how you are changed!"

Harding was talking to Kate while these few words passed, but he heard them; nor did he

fail to remark that two mounted dragoons, ‹
leading a horse by the rein, followed the yo
officer from the wood. He now recognised l
also; and by his dress perceived the rank
held in the army, though Mrs. Clare called l
"Mr. Henry."

"Yes, I am changed, indeed!" replied L
ton, to the widow's last remark, "in body ;
health, Mrs. Clare, but not in heart, I can ass
you; and as I was obliged to visit this wo
I resolved I would not be so near you with
coming in to see how you were going on, w
your pretty Kate here."

"My pretty Kate, very soon!" said Hardi
aloud; and the young officer turned sudde
round, and looked at him more attentively tl
before.

"Ah, Mr. Harding!" he exclaimed, "is t
you? We have met before, though perh
you don't remember me."

"Oh yes, I do, sir," replied the smugg
drily. "But I must go, Kate;" and he add
in a low tone, "I shall be back by-and-by."

Thus saying, he walked away; but before
had taken ten steps, Leyton followed, and to
him by the arm. "What do you want w
me, sir?" asked the smuggler, turning shar

)und, and putting his hand in the bosom of is coat.

" Hush!" replied the young officer; "I seek o harm to you—merely one word. For leaven's sake, Harding, quit this perilous life f yours!—at least, before you marry that poor irl—if I have understood you rightly, that you :e about to marry her. I speak as a friend."

" Thank you, sir!" answered the smuggler, I dare say you mean it kind; but it was ardly fair of you, either, to come and talk with ie upon the cliff, if you are, as I suppose, the ir Henry Leyton all the folks are speaking oout."

" Why, my good friend, my talking with you id you no harm," replied the young officer; you cannot say that I led you to speak of anying that could injure either you or others. Bedes, I have nothing to do with you gentlemen of ie sea, though I may with your friends on land. ut take the advice of one well disposed toards you; and, above all, do not linger about iis place at present, for it is a dangerous eighbourhood for any one who has had a iare in the late transactions."

" That advice I shall take, at all events," iswered Harding, bluntly; " and perhaps the other too, for I am sick of all this!" And tl saying, he walked away, passing close by two dragoons, who offered no obstruction.

In the meanwhile Leyton, returning to Wid Clare and her daughter, went into the cotta and talked to them, for a few minutes, of days. Gradually, however, he brought the c versation round to the inhabitants of Harbou House, and asked if either the widow or K ever went up there.

"Oh, Kate goes twice every day, sir," s Mrs. Clare, "for we have all the finest of poultry to keep down here. But are you going there yourself, Mr. Henry?"

"Alas, no!" answered Leyton, with a si "Those days have gone by, Mrs. Clare; an am now a stranger where I was once loved."

"Don't say so, sir," replied the wid "don't say so! For, I am sure, where you w best loved of all, there you are best loved sti

"That I believe," answered Leyton; "but all events, I am not going there at prese and if Kate would do me a service, she wou the first time she sees Miss Zara Croyla alone, tell her, that if ever she rides or wa out along the road by the Chequers, she will fi an old friend by the way."

"Miss Zara, sir, did you say?" asked Widow Clare.

"Yes, mother—yes," cried Kate; "you forget Miss Edith is not there now; she is down at Mr. Croyland's."

"But remember, Kate," continued Leyton, "I do not wish my name mentioned to many persons in the house. Indeed, it will be better not to speak of me at all to any one but Zara. It must be soon known that I am here, it is true; but I wish to let events take their course till then. And now, Mrs. Clare, good evening. I shall see you again some day soon; and you must let me know when Kate's wedding-day is fixed."

The mother looked at her daughter with a smile, and Kate blushed and laughed. "It is to be this day week, sir," answered Mrs. Clare.

Leyton nodded his head, saying, "I will not forget," and, mounting his horse at the door, rode away.

"Now, did you find him, Kate?" asked Mrs. Clare, in a low tone, the moment Sir Henry Leyton was gone.

"Oh yes," replied her daughter; "the dragoons did not follow me, as you thought they would, mother; and I set down the basket close to the willow. At first he did not answer when I asked if he wanted anything; but when I spoke again, he said, 'No. A thousand thanks for what you have brought;' and he spoke kind and civilly. Then, just as I was going away, he said, 'Kate, Kate! let me know when the soldiers are gone.—If you could bring me a woman's dress, I could easily get away.' I should not be afraid of going any more, mother," the girl continued; "for he seems quite changed by his misfortune, and not rude and jesting as he always used tc be, whenever I saw him before."

The idea of the woman's clothes seemed to strike Mrs. Clare very much; and the good widow and her daughter set their wits to work, to consider how all that was necessary could be procured; for a very serious impediment thrust itself in the way of either mother or child lending him a suit of their own apparel. Neither of them were very tall women; and though young Radford was himself not above the middle height, yet Kate's gown would not have fallen further than half way down his leg; and the poor girl laughed merrily, to think of what a figure he would make dressed in her garments. It would have been the old story of the wolf in sheep's clothing, assuredly.

"If we could but accomplish it, and enable him to escape," thought Mrs. Clare, "especially after Harding has just been up here, it would show Mr. Radford, clearly enough, that John had nothing to do with informing against him." But the question, of where fitting apparel was to be procured, still remained unsettled, till Kate suggested, that perhaps her aunt's, at Glassenbury, might do. "She is very tall," continued the girl, "and I am sure she would lend them to me; for she and my uncle have always been so kind. Suppose I walk over early to-morrow, and ask her."

Now the little farm which Mrs. Clare's brother held, was somewhat more than seven miles off, on the other side of Cranbrook. But still, what is the exertion which woman will not make for a fellow-creature in distress; and Mrs. Clare determined that she would rise betimes, and go to William Harris's herself, certain of a kind reception and ready consent from those who had always displayed towards her, in adversity, the feelings of affection, which the more worldly-minded generally shower upon prosperity alone.

It was far for her daughter to walk, she thought; and besides, Harding might come, and it would not do for Kate to be absent. Thus had she settled it in her own mind, when Mr. Radford entered the cottage to inquire after his son.

High were the praises that he bestowed upon Kate and Mrs. Clare, for their kindness; and he expressed his warm approval of their little scheme. Nevertheless, he turned the matter in his mind, in order to see whether he could not save Mrs. Clare the trouble of going nearly to Goudhurst, by obtaining the necessary articles of female apparel somewhere else. His own women servants, however, were all short and stout; the only other persons whom he could think of, as at all approaching his son in height, he did not choose to trust; and therefore it was, at length, determined that the original plan should be followed. But the worthy gentleman laid strict injunctions upon Mrs. Clare, to be early in her proceedings, as he feared much, from all he had gathered, that the wood might be more strictly searched, in the course of the following day.

When this was settled, and Mr. Radford had expressed his thanks, more than once, Mrs. Clare thought it a good opportunity of turning the conversation to Harding; and she asked Mr.

Radford if he had seen him, adding, "He has gone to look for you, sir, and seems very quick and angry, because the people down about his place have got a report that he informed about the run; and he fancies you have said so."

"Pooh, nonsense, Mrs. Clare, I never said anything of the kind!" replied Mr. Radford. "It is a story put about by the Custom-House officers themselves, just to cover the persons from whom they had the information. But we shall discover them some day, and pay them handsomely. Tell Harding not to mind what people say, for I never thought of such a thing."

"That I will, sir," replied the widow; "for I'm sure it will set his mind at rest.—You must know very well, sir, that he's as honest a man as ever lived."

"To be sure—to be sure," answered Mr. Radford, with great warmth of manner; "no one knows that better than I do, Mrs. Clare."

But whether Mr. Radford really felt the warmth which he assumed, may be another question. His seemings were not always the best indications of his real sentiments; and when he left Mrs. Clare's cottage, after all had been arranged, his first thought was, "We will reckon with Mr. Harding by-and-by.—The account is not made up yet."

Before I proceed to other scenes, it may be as well to go on with the part assigned in this history to Mrs. Clare and her daughter, at least, till the morning of the following day. About eight o'clock at night, Harding returned, still irritable and discontented, having failed to find Mr. Radford. The account, however, which the widow gave of her conversation with that gentleman, soothed him a good deal; but he would not stay the night, as he had done before, saying that he must absolutely be at home as soon as possible, and would return, perhaps, the next day, or, at all events, the day after.

"I must do the best I can, Mrs. Clare," he continued, "to help these fellows out of the scrape they've run into. Two or three of them are good men enough; and, as they risk their necks if they are taken, I should like to get them down, and give them a passage to the other side. So you see I shall be going about here a good deal, for the next four or five days, and will look in, from time to time, to see you and my dear little Kate."

"But are you going to walk all the way back to-night, John?" asked Kate, as he rose to depart.

"No, my love," he answered, "I've got a horse up at Plurendon; but the beast cast a shoe as I was coming, and I was obliged to leave him at the blacksmith's."

No sooner was Harding gone, than a little kindly contest rose between mother and daughter, as to which should go over to Glassenbury; but Mrs. Clare persisted, against all her child's remonstrances; and, in order that they might rise before daylight, both retired to bed early, and slept calmly and peacefully, unknowing what the morrow, to which they both looked anxiously forward, was to bring. The sun was yet some way below the horizon, when Mrs. Clare set out; but she met with no impediment, and, walking on stoutly, arrived, at an early hour, at a little farm-house, inhabited by her brother. She found farmer Harris and his wife, with their two sons and Mrs. Harris's nephew (three stout, good humoured, young men) seated at their breakfast; and warm and joyful was the reception of Aunt Clare; one joking her upon Kate's approaching marriage; another declaring Jack Harding, whom they all knew, was a capital fellow; and all striving to make her comfortable, and pressing her to partake of their morning meal.

Every one of the party was eager to obtain

some information from her, who lived so much nearer to the spot, in regard to the late discomfiture of the smugglers, although none seemed to take any great interest in them, all declaring that the Ramleys, and their gang, were the pest of the country, and that young Dick Radford was not a bit better. Such opinions, regarding that young gentleman, acted as a warning to Mrs. Clare, not to mention the object of the loan she came to solicit; and when, after having rested about twenty minutes, she preferred her petition to Mrs. Harris, it was readily granted by the tall farmer's wife, although not without some expression of curiosity, as to what her sister-in-law could want a dress of hers for.

"Kate or I will bring it back to-night or to-morrow morning," replied Mrs. Clare, "and I'll tell you what we want it for, at the wedding, which, remember, is to be yesterday week."

"Ay, we will all come down with white favours, and our best buckles," said young William, the farmer's eldest son; "and I'll have a kiss of the bride."

A gown and cloak of Mrs. Harris's, having been brought down—they were not her best —and neatly folded up in a shawl-handkerchief, Mrs. Clare set forward on her way home, hurrying her steps as much as possible, lest any untoward event should prevent the execution of her scheme. A stout country woman, accustomed to exercise, the widow accomplished the walk in as short a time as possible; yet it was nine o'clock before she reached the cottage, and she instantly dispatched her daughter to the "hide" in the wood, with the clothes folded up in as small a space as possible, and laid in the bottom of a basket, covered over with eggs.

The only difficulty was, in regard to a bonnet; and, after earnest consultation between mother and child, it was determined that, as Mrs. Clare's head was somewhat larger than Kate's, her bonnet should be put over her daughter's, which was easily accomplished. Both were of straw, and both were plain enough; but, to conceal the contrivance from the eyes of any one whom Kate might meet, Mrs. Clare pinned a small piece of lace—which had been bought for the wedding—into the inside of her own bonnet, remarking, that it would do to hide young Mr. Radford's face a bit.

Furnished with all that was needful, and having had the instructions which Mr. Radford had left, repeated carefully to her, by her mother, fair Kate Clare set out upon her expedition, passing one of the dragoons, who were still patrolling round the wood, near the place where the road entered it. The man said something to her, as she went by, but did not attempt to follow; and Kate walked on, looking behind her, from time to time, till she was satisfied that her proceedings were unwatched. Then, hurrying on, with a quicker step, she turned to the path, which led to the back of the gardens of Harbourne House, and approached the old willow, and the brushwood which covered the place where Richard Radford was concealed.

"Mr. Radford," she said, as soon as she was quite close, "Mr. Radford! Here is what you wanted. Take it as fast as you can."

"Is there any one near but you, Kate?" asked the voice of Richard Radford.

"Oh, no!" she replied; "but the soldiers are still on the outside of the wood watching."

"I know that," rejoined the voice again, "for I saw them last night, when I tried to get out. But are you sure that none of them followed you, Kate?"

"Oh, quite sure," she answered, "for I looked behind all the way!"

"Well, stay and help me to put the things

on," said Richard Radford, issuing forth from behind the bushes, like a snake out of its hole. Kate Clare willingly agreed to help him, and while the gown and the cloak were thrown over his other clothes, told him all that his father had said, desiring him not to come up to Radford Hall till he heard more; but to go down to the *lone house,* near Iden Green, where he would find one or two friends already collected.

"Why, these are never your own clothes, Kate!" said young Radford, as she pinned on the gown for him. "They fit as if they were made for me."

"Not at the back," answered Kate, laughing, "I cannot get the gown to meet there; but that will be covered up by the cloak, so it does not matter.—No, they are my aunt's, at Glassenbury; and you must let me have them back, Mr. Radford, as soon as ever you have got to Iden Green; for my mother has promised to return them to-night."

"I don't know how I shall get them back, Kate," answered Richard Radford; "for none of our people will like to venture up here. Can't you come down and fetch them? It is not much out of your way."

"No, I can't do that," answered Kate, who

did not altogether like going to the lone hous she had mentioned; "but you can send then down to Cranbrook, at all events; and ther they can be left for me, at Mrs. Tims's shop They'll be quite safe; and I will call for then either to-night or to-morrow morning."

"Well, I will do that, my love," replie Richard Radford, taking the bonnet and puttin it on his head.

"Very well, sir," answered Kate, not wel pleased with the epithet he had bestowed upo her, and taking a step to move away, "I wil call for them there."

But young Radford threw his arm round he waist, saying, "Come, Kate! I must have a kis before you go.—You give plenty to Harding, dare say."

"Let me go, sir!" cried Kate Clare, indignantly. "You are a base, ungrateful young man!"

But young Radford did not let her go. He took the kiss she struggled against, by force; and he was proceeding to further insult, when Kate exclaimed, "If you do not let me go, I will scream till the soldiers are upon you.—They are not far."

She spoke so loud, that her very tone excited

his alarm; and he withdrew his arm from her waist, but still held her hand tight, saying, "Come, come, Kate! Nonsense, I did not mean to offend you! Go up to Harbourne House, there's a good girl, and stay as long as you can there, till I get out of the wood."

"You do offend me—you do offend me!" cried Kate Clare, striving to withdraw her hand from his grasp.

"Will you promise to go up to Harbourne, then?" said Richard Radford, "and I will let you go."

"Yes, yes," answered Kate, "I will go;" and the moment her hand was free, she darted away, leaving the basket she had brought behind her.

As soon as she was gone, Richard Radford cursed her for a saucy jade, as if the offence had been hers, not his; and then taking up the basket, he threw it, eggs and all, together with his own hat, into the deep hole in the sand-bank. Advancing along the path till he reached the open road, he hurried on in the direction of Widow Clare's cottage. Of a daring and resolute disposition—for his only virtue was courage—he thought of passing the soldiers, as a good joke rather than a difficult undertaking;

but still recollecting the necessity of caution, a
he came near the edge of the wood he slackene
his pace, tried to shorten his steps, and assume
a more feminine demeanour. When he wa
within a couple of hundred yards of the ope
country, he saw one of the dragoons slowly pas
the end of the road and look up; and, on issuin
forth from the wood, he perceived that the ma
had paused, and was gazing back. But at th
distance, the female garments which he wore de
ceived the soldier; and he was suffered to wal
on unopposed towards Iden Green.

CHAPTER IV.

Sir Robert Croyland himself did not return to Harbourne House, till the hands of the clock pointed out to every one that went through the hall, that it was twenty minutes past the usual dinner hour; and, though he tried to be as expeditious as he could, he was yet fully ten minutes longer in dressing than usual. He was nervous; he was agitated; all the events of that day had shaken and affected him; he was angry with his servant; and several times he gave the most contradictory orders. Although for years he had been undergoing a slow and gradual change, under the painful circumstances in which he had been placed, and had, from the gay, rash, somewhat noisy and overbearing country gentleman, dwindled down into the cold, silent, pompous, and imperative man of family yet the alteration during that day had been so great and peculiar that the valet could no help remarking it, and wondering if his maste was ill.

Sir Robert tried to smoothe his look and compose his manner for the drawing-room however; and when he entered, he gazed round for Sir Edward Digby, observing aloud: "Why I thought soldiers were more punctual. However, as it happens, to-day I am glad Sir Edwar is not down."

"Down!" cried Mrs. Barbara, who had grand objection to dinners being delayed "why, he is out; but you could expect n better; for yesterday you were so long that th fish was done to rags; so I ordered it not to b put in till he made his appearance."

"I told you, my dear aunt, that he said h might not be back before dinner," replied he niece, "and, therefore, it will be vain to wait fo him. He desired me to say so, papa."

"Oh yes! Zara knows all about it," said Mrs Barbara, with a shrewd look; "they were talking together for ten minutes in the library; an I cannot get her to tell me what it was about."

It is, indeed, conscience that makes coward

of us all; and had the fair girl's conversation with her new friend been on any other subject than that to which it related—had it been about love, marriage, arms, or divinity, she would have found no difficulty in parrying her aunt's observations, however mal-à-propos they might have been. At present, however, she was embarrassed by doubts of the propriety of what she was doing, more especially as she felt sure that her father would be inquisitive and suspicious, if the tale the maid had told was true. Acting, however, as she not unfrequently did, in any difficulty, she met Mrs. Barbara's inuendoes at once, replying, "Indeed I shall not say anything about it to any one, my dear aunt. I will manage some matters for myself; and the only thing I shall repeat is Sir Edward's last dying speech, which was to the effect, that he feared he might be detained till after our dinner hour, but would be back as soon as ever he could, and trusted my father would not wait."

"Do you know where he is gone, and why?" asked Sir Robert Croyland, in a much quieter tone than she expected. But poor Zara was still puzzled for an answer; and, as her only resource, she replied vaguely, "Something about some of the smugglers, I believe."

"Then had he any message or intelligence brought him?" inquired Sir Robert Croyland.

"I do not know—Oh, yes, I believe he had," replied his daughter, in a hesitating tone and with a cheek that was beginning to grow red. "He spoke with one of the soldiers at the corner of the road, I know;—and, oh yes, I saw a man ride up with a letter."

"That was after he was gone," observed Mrs. Barbara; but Sir Robert paid little attention, and, ringing, ordered dinner to be served. Could we see into the breasts of others, we should often save ourselves a great deal of unnecessary anxiety. Zara forgot that her father was not as well aware that Sir Edward Digby was Leyton's dearest friend, as she was; but, in truth, all that he concluded—either from the pertinent remarks of Mrs. Barbara or from Zara's embarrassment—was, that the young baronet had been making a little love to his daughter, which, to say sooth, was a consummation that Sir Robert Croyland was not a little inclined to see.

In about a quarter of an hour more, the dinner was announced; and the master of the house, his sister, and Zara, sat down together. Hardly had the fish and soup made any progress, when the quick canter of Sir Edward Digby's horse put his fair confidante out of her anxiety; and, in a few minutes after, he appeared himself, and apologized gracefully to his host, for having been too late. "You must have waited for me, I fear," he added, "for it is near an hour after the time; but I thought it absolutely necessary, from some circumstances I heard, to go over and see my colonel before he returned to Hythe, and then I was detained."

"Pray, who does command your regiment?" asked Mrs. Barbara. But Sir Edward Digby was, at that moment, busily engaged in taking his seat by Zara's side; and he did not hear. The lady repeated the question when he was seated; but then he replied, "No, I thank you, my dear madam, no soup to-day—a solid meal always after a hard ride; and I have galloped till I have almost broken my horse's wind.—By the way, Sir Robert, I hope you found my bay a pleasant goer. I have only ridden him twice since I bought him, though he cost two hundred guineas."

"He is well worth the money," replied the Baronet—"a very powerful animal—bore me like a feather, and I ride a good weight."

"Have your own horses come back?' asked the young officer, with a laugh.

Sir Robert Croyland answered in the negative, adding, "And that reminds me I must write to my brother, to let Edith have his carriage to-morrow, to bring her back; for mine are gone—coach-horses, and all."

"Edith, to-morrow!" exclaimed Mrs. Barbara, in surprise; "why, I thought she was going to stay four or five days."

"She is coming back to-morrow, Bab," replied Sir Robert, sharply; and instantly turned the conversation.

During the rest of the evening, Sir Edward Digby remained very constantly by fair Zara's side; and, moreover, he paid her most particular attention, in so marked a manner, that both Sir Robert Croyland and Mrs. Barbara thought matters were taking their course very favourably. The father busied himself in writing a letter and one or two notes, which he pronounced to be of consequence—as, indeed, they really were—while the aunt, worked diligently and discreetly at embroidering, not interrupting the conference of her niece and their guest above ten times in a minute. Sir Edward, indeed, kept himself within all due and well-defined rules. He never proceeded beyond what a great master of the art has pronounced to be "making love"—"a course of small, quiet, attentions, not so pointed as to alarm, nor so vague as to be misunderstood." Strange to say, Zara was very much obliged to him for following such a course, as it gave an especially good pretext for intimacy, for whispered words and quiet conversation, and even for a little open seeking for each other's society, which would have called observation, if not inquiry, upon them, had not her companion's conduct been what it was. She thought fit to attribute it, in her own mind, entirely to his desire of communicating to her, without attracting notice, whatever he had learned, that could in any way affect her sister's fate; and she judged it a marvellous good device that they should appear for the time as lovers, with full powers on both parts to withdraw from that position whenever it suited them. Poor girl! she knew not how far she was entangling herself.

Sir Edward Digby, in the meanwhile, took no alarming advantage of his situation. The whispered word was almost always of Edith or of Leyton. He never spoke of Zara herself, or of himself, or of his own feelings; not a word could denote to her that he was making love, though his whole demeanour had very much that aspect to those who sat and looked on. Oh, those who sit and look on, what a world they see! and what a world they don't see! Ever more than those who play the game, be they shrewd as they may: ever less than the cards would show, were they turned up. By fits and snatches, he communicated to his fair companion, while he was playing with this ball of gold thread, or winding and unwinding that piece of crimson silk, as much of what had passed between himself and Sir Henry Leyton, as he thought necessary; and then he asked her to sing—as her aunt had given him a quiet hint that her niece did sometimes do such a thing—saying, in a low tone, while he preferred the request, "Pray, go on with the song, though I may interrupt you sometimes with questions, not quite relevant to the subject."

"I understand—I quite understand," answered Zara; but it may be a question whether that sweet girl really quite understood either herself or him. It is impossible that any two free hearts, can go on long, holding such intimate and secret communion, on subjects deeply interesting to both, without being drawn together by closer bonds, than perhaps they fancy can ever be established between them—unless there be something inherently repulsive on one part or the other. Propinquity is certainly much, in the matter of love; but there are circumstances, not rarely occurring in human life, which mightily abridge the process; and such are—difficulties and dangers experienced together—a common struggle for a common object—but more than all—mutual and secret communion with, and aid of each other in things of deep interest. The confidence that is required, the excitement of imagination, the unity of effort, and of purpose, the rapid exercise of mind to catch the half-uttered thought, the enforced candour from want of time, which admits of no disguise or circumlocution, the very mystery itself—all cast that magic chain around those so circumstanced, within which they can hardly escape from the power of love. Nine times out of ten, they never try; and, however Zara Croyland might feel, she rose willingly enough to sing, while Sir Edward Digby leaned over her chair, as she sat at the instrument, which in those days supplied the place of that which is now absurdly enough termed in England, a piano. Her voice, which was fine though not very powerful, wavered a little as she began, from emotions of many kinds. She wished to sing well; but she sang worse than she might have done; yet quite well enough to please Sir Edward Digby, though his ear was refined by art, and good by nature. Nevertheless, though he listened with delight, and felt the music deeply, he forgot not his purpose, and between each stanza asked some question, obtaining a brief reply. But I will not so interrupt the course of an old song, and will give the interrogatory a separate place:

THE LADY'S SONG.

"Oh! there be many, many griefs,
In this world's sad career,
That shun the day, that fly the gaze,
And never, never meet the ear.

But what is darkest—darkest of them all?
The pang of love betray'd?—
The hopes of youth all fleeting by—
Spring flowers that early, early fade?

But there are griefs—ay, griefs as deep:
The friendship turn'd to hate—
And, deeper still—and deeper still,
Repentance come too late!—too late!

The doubt of those we love; and more
The rayless, dull despair,
When trusted hearts are worthless found,
And all our dreams are air—but air.

Deep in each bosom's secret cell,
  The hermit-sorrows lie;
And thence—unheard on earth—they raise
  The voice of prayer on high—on high.

Oh! there be many, many griefs,
  In this world's sad career,
That shun the day, that fly the gaze,
  And, never, never meet the ear."

Thus sang the lady; and one of her hearers, at least, was delighted with the sweet voice, and the sweet music, and the expression which she gave to the whole. But though he listened with deep attention, both to words and tones, as long as her lips moved, yet, when the mere instrumental part of the music recommenced, which was the case between every second and third stanza—and the symphonetic parts of every song were somewhat long in those days—he instantly remembered the object with which he had first asked her to sing, (little thinking that such pleasure would be his reward;) and bending down his head, as if he were paying her some lover-like compliment on her performance, he asked her quietly, as I have said before, a question or two, closely connected with the subject on which both their minds were at that moment principally bent.

Thus, at the first pause, he inquired—"Do you know—did you ever see, in times long past, a gentleman of the name of Warde—a clergyman—a good and clever man, but somewhat strange and wild?"

"No," answered Zara, looking down at the keys of the harpsichord; "I know no one of that name;" and she recommenced the song.

When her voice again ceased, the young officer seemed to have thought further; and he asked, in the same low tone, "Did you ever know a gentleman answering that description—his features must once have been good—somewhat strongly marked, but fine and of an elevated expression, with a good deal of wildness in the eye, but a peculiarly bland and beautiful smile when he is pleased—too remarkable to be overlooked or forgotten?"

"Can you be speaking of Mr. Osborn?" asked Zara, in return. "I barely recollect him in former days; but I and Edith met him about ten days ago; and he remembered and spoke to her."

The song required her attention; and though she would fain have played the symphony over again, she was afraid her father would remark it, and went on to sing the last two stanzas. As soon as she had concluded, however, she said, in a low, quick voice, "He is a very extraordinary man."

"Can you give me any sign by which I should know him?" asked Digby.

"He has now got a number of blue lines traced on his face," answered Zara; "he went abroad to preach to the savages, I have heard. He is a good man, but very eccentric."

At the same moment the voice of her father was raised, saying, "I wish, my dear, you would not sing such melancholy things as that. Cannot you find something gayer? I do not like young ladies singing such dull ditties, only fit for sentimental misses of the true French school."

What was the true French school of his day, I cannot tell. Certainly, it must have been very different from the present.

"Perhaps Sir Edward will sing something more cheerful himself?" answered Zara.

"Oh, I am a very bad musician," replied the young officer; "I cannot even accompany myself. If you will, and have any of the few things I know, I shall be very happy.—In everything, one can but try," he added, in a low voice, "still hoping for the best."

Zara looked over her collection of music with him; and at last she opened one song which was somewhat popular in those times, though it has long fallen into well-merited oblivion. "Can you venture to sing that?" she asked, pointing to the words rather than the music; "it is quite a soldier's song."

Sir Edward Digby read the first line; and thinking he observed a double meaning in her question, he answered, "Oh, yes, that I will, if you will consent to accompany me."

Zara smiled, and sat down to the instrument again; and the reader must judge from the song itself whether the young officer's conjecture that her words had an enigmatical sense was just or not.

THE OFFICER'S SONG.

"A star is still beaming
Beyond the grey cloud;
Its light rays are streaming,
With nothing to shroud;
And the star shall be there
When the clouds pass away;
Its lustre unchanging,
Immortal its ray.

"'Tis the guide of the true heart,
In field, or on sea;
'Tis the hope of the slave,
And the trust of the free;

The light of the lover,
  Whatever assail;
The strength of the honest,
  That never can fail.

" Waft, waft, thou light wind,
  From the peace-giving ray,
The vapours of sorrow,
  That over it stray;
And let it pour forth,
  All unshrouded and bright,
That those who now mourn,
  May rejoice in its light."

"God grant it!" murmured the voice of Sir Robert Croyland. Zara said, "Amen," in her heart; and in a minute or two after, her father rose, and left the room.

During the rest of the evening, nothing very important occurred in Harbourne House. Mrs. Barbara played her usual part, and would contribute to Sir Edward Digby's amusement in a most uncomfortable manner. The following morning, too, went by without any incident of importance, till about ten o'clock, when breakfast just being over, and Zara having been called from the room by her maid, Sir Robert's butler announced to his master, that the groom had returned from Mr. Croyland's.

"Where is the note?" demanded his master, eagerly.

"He has not brought one, Sir Robert," replied the servant, "only a message, sir, to say that Mr. Croyland is very sorry he cannot spare the horses to-day, as they were out a long way yesterday."

Sir Robert Croyland started up in a state of fury not at all becoming. He stamped, he even swore. But we have got rid of a great many of the vices of those times; and swearing was so common at the period I speak of, that it did not even startle Mrs. Barbara. Her efforts, however, to soothe her brother, only served to irritate him the more; and next he swore at her, which did surprise her mightily.

He then fell into a fit of thought, which ended in his saying aloud, "Yes, that must be the way. It is his business, and so——" But Sir Robert did not conclude the sentence, retiring to his own sitting-room, and there writing a letter.

When he had done, he paused and meditated, his mind rambling over many subjects, though still occupied intensely with only one. "I am a most unfortunate man," he thought. "Nothing since that wretched day has ever gone right with me. Even trifles combine to frustrate everything I attempt. Would I had died many years ago! Poor Edith—poor girl—she must know more sorrow still, and yet it must be done, or I am lost!—If that wretched youth had been killed in that affray yesterday, it would have all been over. Was there no bullet that could find him?—and yet, perhaps, it might not have had the effect.—No, no; there would have been some new kind of demand from that greedy, craving scoundrel.—May there not be such even now? Will he give up that fatal paper?—He shall—by Heaven, he shall!—But I must send the letter. Sir Edward Digby will think this all very strange. How unfortunate, that it should have happened just when he was here. Would to Heaven I had any one to consult with! But I am lone, lone indeed. My wife, my sons, my friends,—gone, gone, all gone! It is very sad;" and after having mused for several minutes more, he rang the bell, gave the servant who appeared the letter which he had just written, and directed him to take it over to Mr. Radford's as soon as possible.

Returning to the room which he had previously left—without bestowing one word upon Mrs. Barbara, whom he passed in the corridor, Sir Robert Croyland entered into conversation with Sir

Edward Digby, and strove—though with too evident an effort—to appear careless and unconcerned.

In the meantime, however, we must notice what was passing in the corridor; for it was of some importance, though, like many other important things, it was transacted very quietly.

Mrs. Barbara had overheard Sir Robert's directions to the servant; and she had seen the man—as he went away to get ready the pony, which was usually sent in the morning to the post—deposit the note he had received upon an antique piece of furniture—a large marble table, with great sprawling gilt legs—which stood in the hall, close to the double doors that led to the offices.

Now, Mrs. Barbara was one of the most benevolent people upon earth: she literally overflowed with the milk of human kindness; and, if a few drops of that same milk occasionally spotted the apron of her morality, which we cannot help acknowledging was sometimes the case, she thought, as a great many other people do of a great many other sins, that "there was no great harm in it, if the motive was good." This was one of those cases and occasions when the milk was beginning to run over. She had a deep regard for her brother: she would have sacrificed her right hand for him; and she was quite sure that something very sad had happened to vex him, or he never would have thought of swearing *at her.* She would have done, she was ready to do, anything in the world, to help him; but how could she help him, without knowing what he was vexed about? It is wonderful how many lines the devil always has out, for those who are disposed to take a bait. Something whispered to Mrs. Barbara, as she gazed at the letter, "The whole story is in there!" Ah, Mrs. Barbara, do not take it up, and look at the address!—It is dangerous—very dangerous.

But Mrs. Barbara did take it up, and looked at the address—and then at the two ends. It was folded as a note, unfortunately; and she thought—"There can be no harm, I'm sure—I won't open it—though I've seen him open Edith's letters, poor thing!—I shall hear the man pull back the inner door, and can put it down in a minute. Nobody else can see me here; and if I could but find out what is vexing him, I might have some way of helping him; I'm sure I intend well."

All this argumentation in Mrs. Barbara's

mind took up the space of about three seconds; and then the note, pressed between two fingers in the most approved fashion, was applied as a telescope to her eye, to get a perspective view of the cause of her brother's irritation. I must make the reader a party to the transaction, I am afraid, and let him know the words which Mrs. Barbara read :—

"My dear Radford," the note began—"As misfortune would have it, all my horses have been taken out of the stable, and have not been brought back. I fear that they have fallen into other hands than those that borrowed them; and my brother Zachary has one of his crabbed moods upon him, and will not lend his carriage to bring Edith back. If your horses have not gone as well as mine, I should feel particularly obliged by your sending them down here, to take over my coach to Zachary's and bring Edith back; for I do not wish her to stay there any longer, as the marriage is to take place so soon. If you can come over to-morrow, we can settle whether it is to be at your house or here—though I should prefer it here, if you have no objection."

There seemed to be a few words more; but it took Mrs. Barbara longer to decipher the above lines, in the actual position of the note, than it might have done, had the paper been spread out fair before her; so that, just as she was moving it a little, to get at the rest, the sound of the farther of the two doors being thrown open, interrupted her proceedings; and, laying down the letter quickly, she darted away, full of the important intelligence which she had acquired.

CHAPTER V.

THERE are periods in the life of some men, when, either by a concatenation of unfortunate events, or by the accumulated consequences of their own errors, the prospect on every side becomes so clouded, that there is no resource for them, but to shut their eyes to the menacing aspect of all things, and to take refuge in the moral blindness of thoughtless inaction, against the pressure of present difficulties. "I dare not think," is the excuse of many a man, for continuing in the same course of levity which first brought misfortunes upon him; but such is not always the case with those who fly to wretched merriment in the hour of distress; and such was not the case with Sir Robert Croyland.

He had thought for long years, till his very

heart sickened at the name of reflection. He had looked round for help, and had found none. He had tried to discover some prospect of relief; and all was darkness. The storm he had long foreseen was now bursting upon his head; it was no longer to be delayed; it was not to be warded off. His daughter's misery, or his own destruction, was the only choice before him; and he was resolved to think no more—to let events take their course, and to meet them as he best might.

But to resolve is one thing—to execute, another; and Edith's father was not a man who could keep such a determination long. He might indeed, for a time, cease to think of all the painful particulars of his situation; but there will ever come moments when thought is forced even upon the thoughtless, and events will arise, to press reflection upon any heart. His efforts were, at first, very successful. After he had despatched the letter to Mr. Radford, he had said, "I must really pay my visitor some attention. It will serve to occupy my mind, too. Anything to escape from the torturing consideration of questions, which must ever be solved in wretchedness." And when he returned to Sir Edward Digby, his conversation was particularly gay and cheerful. It first turned to the unpleasant fact of the abstraction of all his horses; but he now spoke of it in a lighter and less careful manner than before.

"Doubtless," he said, "they have been taken without leave, as usual, by the smugglers, to use for their own purposes. It is quite a common practice in this county; and yet we all go on leaving our stable-doors open, as if to invite all who pass to enter, and choose what they like. Then, I suppose, they have been captured with other spoil, in the strife of yesterday morning, and are become the prize of the conquerors; so that I shall never see them again."

"Oh, no!" answered the young officer, "they will be restored, I am quite sure, upon your identifying them, and proving that they were taken, without your consent, by the smugglers. I shall go over to Woodchurch by-and-by; and if you please, I will claim them for you."

"It is scarcely worth while," replied the baronet; "I doubt that I shall ever get them back. These are little losses which every man in this neighbourhood must suffer, as a penalty for remaining in a half savage part of the country. —What are you disposed to do this morning, Sir Edward? Do you again walk the stubbles?"

"I fear it would be of little use," answered Digby; "there has been so much galloping lately, that I do not think a partridge has been left undisturbed in its furrow; and the sun is too high for much sport."

"Well, then, let us walk in the garden for a little," said Sir Robert; "it is curious, in some respects, having been laid out long before this house was built, antiquated as it is."

Sir Edward Digby assented, but looked round for Zara, as he certainly thought her society would be a great addition to her father's. She had not yet returned to the room, however; and Sir Robert, as if he divined his young companion's feelings, requested his sister to tell her niece, when she came, that he and their guest were walking in the garden. "It is one of her favourite spots, Sir Edward," he continued, as they went out, "and many a meditative hour she spends there; for, gay as she is, she has her fits of thought, too."

The young baronet internally said, "Well she may, in this house!" but making a more civil answer to his entertainer, he followed him to the garden; and so well and even cheerfully did Sir Robert Croyland keep up the conversation, so learnedly did he descant upon the levelling and preservation of turf in bowling-greens, and upon the clipping of old yew-trees—both before and after Zara joined them—that Digby began to doubt, notwithstanding all he had heard, whether he could really have such a load upon his heart as he himself had stated to Edith, and to fancy that, after all, it might be a stratagem to drive her to compliance with his wishes.

A little incident, of no great moment in the eyes of any one but a very careful observer of his fellow-men—and Digby was far more so than he seemed—soon settled the doubt. As they were passing under an old wall of red brick—channelled by time and the shoots of pears and peaches—which separated the garden from the different courts, a door suddenly opened behind them, just after they had passed it; and while Sir Edward's eyes were turned to the face of the master of the house, Sir Robert's ear instantly caught the sound, and his cheek became as pale as ashes.

"There is some dark terror there!" thought the young officer; but, turning to Zara, he finished the sentence he had been uttering, while her father's coachman, who was the person that had opened the door, came forward to say that one of the horses had returned.

"Returned!" exclaimed Sir Robert Croyland; "has been brought back, I suppose you mean?"

"Ay, Sir Robert," replied the man; "a fellow from the lone house by Iden Green brought him; and in a sad state the poor beast is. He's got a cut, like with a knife, all down his shoulder."

"Your dragoon swords are sharp, Sir Edward," said the old baronet, gaily, to his guest; "however, I will go and see him myself, and rejoin you here in a minute."

"I am so glad to have a moment alone," cried Zara, as soon as her father was gone, "that you must forgive me if I use it directly. I am going to ask you a favour, Sir Edward. You must take me a ride, and lend me a horse. I have just had a message from poor Harry Leyton; he wishes to see me, but I am afraid to go alone, with so many soldiers about."

"Are they such terrible animals?" asked her companion, with a smile, adding, however, "I shall be delighted, if your father will consent; for I have already told him that I am going to Woodchurch this afternoon."

"Oh! you must ask me yourself, Sir Edward," replied Zara, "quite in a civil tone; and then when you see that I am willing, you must be very pressing with my father—quite as if you were a lover; and he will not refuse you.—I'll bear you harmless, as I have heard Mr. Radford say;" she added, with a playful smile that was quickly saddened.

"You shall command for the time," answered Digby, as gaily; "perhaps after that, I may take my turn, sweet lady. But I have a good deal to say to you, too, which I could not fully explain last night."

"As we go—as we go," replied Zara; "my father will be back directly, otherwise I would tell you a long story about my aunt, who has evidently got some great secret which she is all impatience to divulge. If I had stayed an hour with her, I might have arrived at it; but I was afraid of losing my opportunity here.—Oh, that invaluable thing, opportunity! Once lost, what years of misery does it not sometimes leave behind.—Would to Heaven that Edith and Leyton had run away with each other when they were about it.—We should all have been happier now."

"And I should never have known you," replied Digby. Zara smiled, and shook her head, as if saying, "That is hardly fair;" but Sir Robert Croyland was seen coming up the walk; and she only replied, "Now do your *devoir,* gallant knight, and let me see if you do it zealously."

"I have been trying in your absence, my dear sir," said Digby, rather maliciously, as the baronet joined them, "to persuade your fair daughter to run away with me. But she is very dutiful, and will not take such a rash step, though the distance is only to Woodchurch, without your consent. I pray you give it; for I long to mount her on my quietest horse, and see her try her skill in horsemanship again."

Sir Robert Croyland looked grave; and ere the words were half spoken, Sir Edward Digby felt that he had committed an error in his game; for he was well aware that when we have a favour to ask, we should not call up, by speech or look, in the mind of the person who is to grant it, any association having a contrary tendency.

"I am afraid that I have no servant whom I could send with you, Sir Edward," replied her father; "one I have just dispatched to some distance, and you know I am left without horses, for this poor beast just come back, is unfit. Neither do I think it would be altogether consistent with decorum, for Zara to go with you quite alone."

Sir Edward Digby mentally sent the word decorum back to the place from whence it came; but he was resolved to press his point; and when Zara replied, "Oh, do let me go, papa!" he added, "My servant can accompany us, to satisfy propriety, Sir Robert; and you know I have quartered three horses upon you. Then, as I find the fair lady is somewhat afraid of a multitude of soldiers, I promise most faithfully not even to dismount in Woodchurch, but to say what I have to say, to the officer in command there, and then canter back over the country."

"Who is the officer in command?" asked Sir Robert Croyland.

Zara drew her breath quick, but Sir Edward Digby avoided the dangerous point. "Irby has one troop there," he replied; "and there are parts of two others. When I have made interest enough here," he continued, with a half bow to Zara, "I shall beg to introduce Irby to you, Sir Robert; you will like him much, I think. I have known him long."

"Pray invite him to dinner while he stays," said Sir Robert Croyland; "it will give me much pleasure to see him."

"Not yet—not yet!" answered Digby, laughing; "I always secure my own approaches first."

Sir Robert Croyland smiled graciously, and, turning to Zara, said, "Well, my dear, I see no objection, if you wish it. You had better go and get ready."

Zara's cheek was glowing, and she took her father at the first word; but when she was gone, Sir Robert thought fit to lecture his guest a little, upon the bad habit of spoiling young ladies which he seemed to have acquired. He did it jocularly, but with his usual pompous and grave air; and no one would have recognised in the Sir Robert Croyland walking in the garden, the father whom we have lately seen humbled before his own child. There is no part of a man's character which he keeps up so well to the world as that part which is not his own. The assertion may seem to be a contradiction in terms; but there is no other way of expressing the sense clearly; and whether those terms be correct or not, will depend upon whether character is properly innate or accumulated.

Sir Edward Digby answered gaily, for it was his object to keep his host in good humour—at least, for the time. He denied the possibility of spoiling a lady, while he acknowledged his propensity to attempt impossibilities in that direction; and at the same time, with a good grace, and a frankness, real yet assumed—for his words were true, though they might not have been spoken just then, under any other circumstances—he admitted that, of all people whom he should like to spoil, the fair being who had just left them was the foremost. The words were too decided to be mistaken. Sir Edward Digby was evidently a gentleman, and known to be a man of honour. No man of honour trifles with a woman's affections;. and Sir Robert Croyland, wise in this instance if not in others, did as all wise fathers would do, held his tongue for a time that the matter might cool and harden, and then changed the subject.

Digby, however, had grown thoughtful. Did he repent what he had said? No, certainly not. He wished, indeed, that he had not been driven to say it so soon; for there were doubts in his own mind whether Zara herself were altogether won. She was frank, she was kind, she trusted him, she acted with him; but there was at times a shade of reserve about her, coming suddenly, which seemed to him as a warning. She had from the first taken such pains to ensure that her confidence—the confidence of circumstances—should not be misunderstood; she had responded so little to the first approaches of love, while she had yielded so readily to those of friendship, that there was a doubt in his mind which made him uneasy; and, every now and then, her uncle's account of her character rung in his ear, and made him think—"I have found this artillery more dangerous than I expected."

What a pity it is that uncles will not hold their tongues!

At length, he bethought him that it would be as well to order the horses, which was accordingly done; and some time before they were ready, the fair girl herself appeared, and continued walking up and down the garden with her father and their guest, looking very lovely, both from excitement, which gave a varying colour to her cheek, and from intense feelings, which, denied the lips, looked out with deeper soul from the eyes.

"I think, Zara," said Sir Robert Croyland, when it was announced that the horses and the servant were ready, "that you took Sir Edward to the north, when you went over to your uncle's.

You had better, therefore, in returning—for I know, in your wild spirits, when once on horseback, you will not be contented with the straight road—you had better, I say, come by the southwest."

"Oh, papa, I could never learn the points of the compass in my life!" answered Zara, laughing; "I suppose that is the reason why, as my aunt says, I steer so ill."

"I mean—by the lower road," replied her father; and he laid such emphasis on the words, that Zara received them as a command.

They mounted and set out, much to the surprise of Mrs. Barbara Croyland, who saw them from the window, and thence derived her first information of their intended expedition; for Zara was afraid of her aunt's kindnesses, and never encountered them when she could help it. When they were a hundred yards from the house, the conversation began; but I will not enter into all the details; for at first they related to facts with which the reader is already well acquainted. Sir Edward Digby told her at large, all that had passed between himself and Leyton on the preceding day, and Zara, in return, informed him of the message she had received from his friend, and how it had been conveyed.

Their minds then turned to other things, or rather to other branches of the same subjects; and, what was to be done? was the next question; for hours were flying—the moment that was to decide the fate of the two beings in whom each felt a deep though separate interest, was approaching fast; and no progress had apparently been made.

Zara's feelings seemed as much divided as Edith's had been. She shrank from the thought, that her sister, whom she loved with a species of adoration, should sacrifice herself on any account to such a fate as that which must attend the wife of Richard Radford. She shrank also, as a young, generous woman's heart must ever shrink, from the thought of any one wedding the abhorred, and separating for ever from the beloved; but then, when she came to turn her eyes towards her father, she trembled for him as much as for Edith; and, with her two hands resting on the pommel of the saddle, she gazed down in anxious and bitter thought.

"I know not your father as well as you do, my dear Miss Croyland," said her companion, at length, as he marked these emotions; "and therefore I cannot tell what might be his conduct under particular circumstances." Zara suddenly raised her eyes, and fixed them on his face; but Digby continued. "I do not speak of the past, but of the future. I take it for granted—not alone as a courtesy, but from all I have seen—that Sir Robert Croyland cannot have committed any act, that could justly render him liable to danger from the law."

"Thank you—thank you!" said Zara, dropping her eyes again; "you judge rightly, I am sure."

"But at the same time," he proceeded, "it is clear that some unfortunate concurrence of circumstances has placed him either really, or in imagination, in Mr. Radford's power. Now, would he but act a bold and decided part—dare the worst—discountenance a bad man and a villain—even, if necessary, in his magisterial capacity, treat him as he deserves—he would take away the sting from his malice. Any accusation this man might bring would have *enmity* too strongly written upon it, to carry much weight; and all the evidence in favour of your father would have double force."

"He cannot—he will not," answered Zara, sadly, "unless he be actually driven. I know no more than you, Sir Edward, how all this has happened; but I know my father, and I know that he shrinks from disgrace more than death. An accusation, a public trial, would kill him by the worst and most terrible kind of torture. Mr. Radford, too, has wound the toils round him completely—that I can see. He could say that Sir Robert Croyland has acted contrary to all his own principles, at his request; and he could point to the cause. He could say that Sir Robert Croyland suddenly became, and has been for years the most intimate friend and companion of a man he scorned and avoided; and he could assert that it was because the proud man was in the cunning man's power. If, for vengeance, he chooses to avow his own disgrace —and what is there not Mr. Radford would avow to serve his ends?—believe me, he has my father in a net, from which it will be difficult to disentangle him."

They both fell into thought again; but Zara did not sink in Digby's estimation, from the clear and firm view which she took of her father's position.

"Well," he said, at length, "let us wait, and hear what poor Leyton has to tell you. Perhaps he may have gained some further insight, or may have formed some plan; and now, Zara, let us for a moment speak of ourselves. You see, to-day, I have been forced to make love to you."

"Too much," said Zara, gravely. "I am sure you intended it for the best; but I am sorry it could not be avoided."

"And yet it is very pleasant," answered Digby, half jestingly, half seriously.

Zara seemed agitated: "Do not, do not!" she replied; "my mind is too full of sad things, to think of what might be pleasant or not at another time;" and she turned a look towards him, in which kindness, entreaty, and seriousness were all so blended, that it left him in greater doubt than ever, as to her sensations. "Besides," she added, the serious predominating in her tone, "consider what a difference one rash word, on either part, may make between us. Let me regard you, at least for the present, as a friend—or a brother, as you once said, Digby; let me take counsel with you, seek your advice, call for your assistance, without one thought or care to shackle or restrain me. In pity, do; for you know not how much I need support."

"Then I am most ready to give it, on your own terms, and in your own way," answered Digby, warmly; but, immediately afterwards, he fell into a reverie, and in his own mind thought—"She is wrong in her view; or indifferent towards me. With a lover to whom all is acknowledged, and with whom all is decided, she would have greater confidence, than with a friend, towards whom the dearest feelings of the heart are in doubt. This must be resolved speedily, but not now; for it evidently agitates her too much.—Yet, after all, in that agitation is hope."

Just as his meditations had reached this point, they passed by the little public house of the Chequers, then a very favourite sign in England, and especially in that part of the country; and in five minutes after, they perceived a horseman on the road, riding rapidly towards them.

"There is Leyton," said Sir Edward Digby, as he came somewhat nearer; but Zara gazed forward with surprise, at the tall, manly figure, dressed in the handsome uniform of the time, the pale but noble countenance, and the calm commanding air. "Impossible!" she cried. "Why, he was a gay, slight, florid, young man."

"Six or seven years ago," answered Digby; "but that, my dear Miss Croyland, is Sir Henry Leyton, depend upon it."

Now, it may seem strange that Edith should have instantly recognised, even at a much greater distance, the man whom her sister did not, though the same period had passed since each had seen him; but, it must be remembered, that Edith was between two and three years older than Zara; and those two or three years, at the time of life which they had reached when Leyton left England, are amongst the most important in a woman's life—those when new feelings and new thoughts arise, to impress for ever, on the woman's heart, events and persons that the girl forgets in an hour.

Leyton, however, it certainly was; and when Zara could see his features distinctly, she recalled the lines. Springing from his horse as soon as he was near, her sister's lover cast the bridle of his charger over his arm, and, taking the hand she extended to him, kissed it affectionately: "Oh, Zara, how you are changed!" he said. "But so am I; and you have gained, whilst I have lost. It is very kind of you to come thus speedily."

"You could not doubt, Leyton, that I would, if possible," answered Zara; "but all things are much changed in our house, as well as ourselves; and that wild liberty which we formerly enjoyed, of running whithersoever we would, is sadly abridged now. But what have you to say, Leyton? for I dare not stay long."

Digby was dropping behind, apparently to speak to his servant for a moment; but Leyton called to him, assuring him that he had nothing to say, which he might not hear.

"Presently, presently," answered Zara's companion; and leaving them alone, he rode up to good Mr. Somers, who, with his usual discretion, had halted, as they halted, at a very respectful distance. The young officer seemed to give some orders, which were rather long, and then returned at a slow pace. In the meantime, the conversation of Leyton and Zara had gone on; but his only object, it appeared, was to see her, and to entreat her to aid and support his Edith in any trial she might be put to. "I spent a short period of chequered happiness with her last night," he said; "and she then told me, dear Zara, that she was sure her father would send for her in the course of this day. If such be the case, keep with her always as far as possible; bid her still remember Harry Leyton; bid her resist to the end; and assure her that he will come to her deliverance ultimately. Were it myself alone, I would sacrifice anything, and set her free; but when I know that, by so doing, I should make her wretched for ever—that her own heart would be broken, and nothing but an early death relieve her, I cannot do it, Zara—no one can expect it."

"Perhaps not—perhaps not, Leyton;" answered Zara, with the tears in her eyes; "but yet—my father! However, I cannot advise—I cannot even ask anything. All is so dark and perplexed, I am lost!"

"I am labouring now, dear Zara," replied the young officer, "to find or devise means of rendering his safety sure. Already I have the power to crush the bad man in whose grasp he is, and render his testimony, whatever it may be, nearly valueless. At all events, the only course before us, is that which I have pointed out; and while Digby is with you, you can never want the best and surest counsel and assistance. You may confide in him fully, Zara. I have now known him many years; and a more honourable and upright man, or one of greater talent, does not live."

There was something very gratifying to Zara in what he said of his friend; and had she been in a mood to scrutinize her own feelings accurately, the pleasure that she experienced in hearing such words spoken of Sir Edward Digby—the agitated sort of pleasure—might have given her an insight into her own heart. As it was, it only sent a passing blush into her cheek, and she replied, "I am sure he is all you say, Harry; and indeed, it is to his connivance that I owe my being able to come hither to-day. These smugglers took away all my father's horses; and I suppose, from what I hear, that some of them have been captured by your men."

"If such is the case they shall be sent back," replied Leyton; "for I am well aware that the horses being found with the smugglers, is no proof that they were there with the owner's consent. To-morrow, I trust to be able to give you a further insight into my plans, for I am promised some information of importance to-night; and perhaps, even before you reach home, I shall have put a bar against Mr. Richard Radford's claims to Edith, which he may find insurmountable."

As he was speaking, Sir Edward Digby returned, quickening his horse's pace as he came near, and pointing with his hand. "You have got a detachment out, I see, Leyton," he said—"Is there any new affair before you?"

"Oh, no," replied the Colonel, "it is merely Irby and a part of his troop, whom I have despatched to search the wood, for I have certain intelligence that the man we are seeking is concealed there."

"They may save themselves the trouble," replied Zara, shaking her head; "for though he was certainly there all yesterday, he made his escape this morning."

Leyton bit his lip, and his brow grew clouded. "That is unfortunate," he said, "most unfortunate!—I do not ask you how you know, Zara; but are you quite sure?"

"Perfectly," she answered—"I would not deceive you for the world, Leyton; and I only say what I have said, because I think that, if you do search the wood, it may draw attention to your being in this neighbourhood, which as yet is not known at Harbourne, and it may embarrass us very much."

"I am not sure, Leyton," said Sir Edward Digby, "that as far as your own purposes are concerned, it might not be better to seem, at all events, to withdraw the troops, or at least a part of them, from this neighbourhood. Indeed, though I have no right to give you advice upon the subject, I think also it might be beneficial in other respects, for as soon as the smugglers think you gone, they will act with more freedom."

"I propose to do so, to-morrow," replied the colonel; "but I have some information already, and expect more, upon which I must act in the first place. It will be as well, however, to stop Irby's party, if there is no end to be obtained by their proceedings."

He then took leave of Zara and his friend, mounted his horse, and rode back to meet the troop that was advancing; while Zara and Sir Edward Digby, after following the same road up to the first houses of Woodchurch, turned away to the right, and went back to Harbourne, by the small country road which leads from Kennardington to Tenterden.

Their conversation, as they went, would be of very little interest to the reader; for it consisted almost altogether of comments upon Leyton's changed appearance, and discussions of the same questions of doubt and difficulty which had occupied them before. They went slowly, however; and when they reached the house it did not want much more than three quarters of an hour to the usual time of dinner. Sir Robert Croyland they found looking out of the glass-door, which commanded a view towards his brother's house, and his first question was, which way they had returned. Sir Edward Digby gave an easy and unconcerned reply, describing the road they had followed, and comparing it, greatly to its disadvantage, with that which they had pursued on their former expedition.

"Then you saw nothing of the carriage, Zara?" inquired her father. "It is very strange that Edith has not come back."

"No, we saw no carriage of any kind; but a carrier's cart," replied the young lady. "Perhaps if Edith did not know you were going to send, she might not be ready."

This reason, however, did not seem to satisfy Sir Robert Croyland; and after talking with him for a few minutes more as he stood, still gazing forth over the country, Zara and Digby retired to change their dress before dinner; and the latter received a long report from his servant of facts which will be shown hereafter. The man was particularly minute and communicative, because his master asked him no questions, and suffered him to tell his tale his own way. But that tale fully occupied the time till the second bell rang, and Digby hurried down to dinner.

Still, Miss Croyland had not returned; and it

was evident that Sir Robert Croyland was annoyed and uneasy. All the suavity and cheerfulness of the morning was gone; for one importunate source of care and thought will always carry the recollection back to others; and he sat at the dinner table in silence and gloom, only broken by brief intervals of conversation, which he carried on with a laborious effort.

Just as Mrs. Barbara rose to retire, however, the butler re-entered the room, announcing to Sir Robert Croyland that Mr. Radford had called, and wished to speak with him. "He would not come in, sir," continued the man, "for he said he wanted to speak with you alone, so I showed him into the library."

Sir Robert Croyland instantly rose, but looked with a hesitating glance at his guest, while Mrs. Barbara and Zara retired from the room.

"Pray, do not let me detain you, Sir Robert," said the young officer; "I have taken as much wine as I ever do, and will go and join the ladies in the drawing room."

The customs of the day required that the master of the house should press the bottle upon his guest; and Sir Robert Croyland did not fail to do so. But Digby remained firm, and, to settle the question, walked quietly to the door and entered the drawing-room. There, he found Zara seated; but Mrs. Barbara was standing near the table, and apparently in a state, for which the English language supplies but one term, and that not a very classical one. I mean, she was in *a fidget*.

The reader is aware that the library of Harbourne House was adjacent to the drawing-room, and that there was a door between them. It was a thick, solid, oaken door, however, such as shut out the wind in the good old times; and, moreover, it fitted very close. Thus, though the minute after Sir Edward had entered the room, a low murmur, as of persons speaking somewhat loud, was heard from the library, not a single syllable could be distinguished; and Mrs. Barbara looked at the keyhole, with a longing indescribable. After about thirty seconds' martyrdom, Mrs. Barbara quitted the room: Zara, who knew her aunt, candidly trusting, that she had gone to put herself out of temptation; and Sir Edward Digby never for a moment imagining, that she could have been in any temptation at all. It may now be necessary, however, to follow Sir Robert Croyland to the library, and to reveal to the reader all that Mrs. Barbara was so anxious to learn.

He found Mr. Radford, booted and spurred, standing, with his tall, bony figure, in as easy an attitude as it could assume, by the fire-place; and the baronet's first question was, "In the name of Heaven, Radford, what has become of Edith?—Neither she nor the carriage have returned."

"Oh, yes, the carriage has, half an hour ago!" replied Mr. Radford; "and I met the horses going back as I came.—Didn't you get my message which I sent by the coachman?"

"No, I must have been at dinner," answered Sir Robert Croyland, "and the fools did not give it to me."

"Well, it is no great matter," rejoined Mr. Radford, in the quietest possible tone. "It was only to say that I was coming over, and would explain to you all about Miss Croyland."

"But where is she? Why did she not come?" demanded her father, with some of the old impetuosity of his youth.

"She is at my house," answered the other, deliberately; "I thought it would be a great deal better, Croyland, to bring her there at once, as you left to me the decision of where the marriage was to be. She could be quite as comfortable there as here. My son will be up to-morrow; and the marriage can take place quietly, without any piece of work. Now, here it would be difficult to manage it; for, in the first place, it would be dangerous for my son. You have got a stranger in the house, and a whole heap of servants, who cannot be trusted. I have arranged everything for the marriage, and for their going off quietly on their little tour. We shall soon get a pardon for this affair with the dragoons; and that will be all settled."

Sir Robert Croyland had remained mute; not with any calm or tranquil feelings, but with indignation and astonishment. "Upon my life and soul," he cried, "this is too bad! Do you mean to say, sir, that you have ventured, without my knowledge or consent, to change my daughter's destination, and take her to your house when I wished her to be brought here?"

"Undoubtedly," replied Mr. Radford, with the most perfect calmness.

"Well then, sir," exclaimed the baronet, irritated beyond all endurance—"I have to tell you, that you have committed a gross, insolent, and unjustifiable act; and I have to insist that she be brought back here this very night."

"Nay, my dear friend—nay," replied Mr. Radford, in a half jeering tone. "These are harsh words that you use; but you must hear me first, before I pay any attention to them."

"I want to hear nothing, sir," cried Sir Robert Croyland, his anger still carrying him forward. "But if you do not send her back to her own home, I will get horses over from Tenterden, and bring her myself.—Her slavery has not yet commenced, Mr. Radford."

"I shall not be able to bring her over," answered Mr. Radford, still maintaining the same provoking coolness; "because, in case of her return, I should be obliged to use my horses myself, to lay certain important facts, which we both know of, before a brother magistrate."

He paused, and Sir Robert Croyland winced. But still indignation was uppermost for the time; and rapidly as lightning the thoughts of resistance passed through his mind. "This man's conduct is too bad," he said to himself. "After such a daring act as this, with his character blackened by so many stains, and so clear a case of revenge, the magistrates will surely hardly listen to him." But as he continued to reflect, timidity—the habitual timidity of many years—began to mingle with and dilute his resolution; and Mr. Radford, who knew him to the very heart, after having suffered him to reflect just long enough to shake his firmness, went on in a somewhat different tone, saying, "Come, Sir Robert! don't be unreasonable; and before you quarrel irretrievably with an old friend, listen quietly to what he has got to say."

"Well, sir, well," said Sir Robert Croyland, casting himself into a chair—"what is it you have got to say?"

"Why, simply this, my dear friend," answered Mr. Radford, "that you are not aware of all the circumstances, and therefore cannot judge yet whether I have acted right or wrong. You and I have decided, I think, that there can no longer be any delay in the arrangement of our affairs. I put it plainly to you yesterday, that it was to be now or never; and you agreed that it should be now. You brought me your daughter's consent in the afternoon; and so far the matter was settled. I don't want to injure you; and if you are injured, it is your own fault—"

"But I gave no consent," said Sir Robert Croyland, "that she should be taken to your house. The circumstances—the circumstances, Mr. Radford!"

"Presently, presently," replied his companion. "I take it for granted, that, when you have pledged yourself to a thing, you are anxious to accomplish it. Now I tell you, there was no sure way of accomplishing this, but that which I have taken. Do you know who is the commander of this dragoon regiment which is down here?—No. But I do. Do you know who is the man, who, like a sub-officer of the Customs, attacked our friends yesterday morning, took some fifty of them prisoners, robbed me of some seventy thousand pounds, and is now hunting after my son, as if he were a fox?—No. But I do; and I will tell you who he is.—One Harry Leyton, whom you may have heard of—now, Lieutenant-Colonel Sir Henry Leyton, Knight of the Bath, forsooth!"

Sir Robert Croyland gazed upon him in astonishment; but, whatever were his other sensations, deep grief and bitter regret mingled with them, when he thought that circumstances should ever have driven or tempted him to promise his daughter's hand to a low, dissolute, unprincipled villain, and to put a fatal barrier between her and one whom he had always known to be generous, honourable, and high principled, and who had now gained such distinction in the service of his country. He remained perfectly silent, however; and the expression of surprise and consternation which his countenance displayed, was misinterpreted by Mr. Radford to his own advantage.

"Now, look here, Sir Robert," he continued; "if your daughter were in your house, you could not help this young man having some communication with her. He has already been over at your brother's, and has seen her, I doubt not. Here, then, is your fair daughter Miss Zara, your guest Sir Edward Digby—his intimate friend, I dare say—all your maids and half your men servants, even dear Mrs. Barbara herself, with her sweet meddling ways, would all be ready to fetch and carry between the lovers. In short, our whole plans would be overturned; and I should be compelled to do that which would be very disagreeable to me, and to strike at this upstart Henry Leyton through the breast of Sir Robert Croyland. In my house, he can have no access to her; and though some mischief may already have been done, yet it can go no further."

"Now I understand what you mean by revenge," said the baronet, in a low tone, folding his hands together.—"Now I understand."

"Well, but have I judged rightly or wrongly?" demanded Mr. Radford.

"Rightly, I suppose," said Sir Robert Croyland, sadly. "It can't be helped;—but poor Edith, how does she bear it?"

"Oh, very well," answered Mr. Radford, quietly. "She cried a little at first, and when she found where they were going, asked the coachman what he meant. It was my coachman, you know, not yours; and so he lied, like a good, honest fellow, and said you were waiting for her at my house. I was obliged to make up a little bit of a story too, and tell her you knew all about it; but that was no great harm; for I was resolved, you should know all about it, very soon."

"Lied like a good honest fellow!" murmured Sir Robert Croyland, to himself. "Well," he continued, aloud, "at all events I must come over to-morrow, and try to reconcile the poor girl to it."

"Do so, do so," answered Mr. Radford; "and in the meantime, I must be off; for I've still a good deal of work to do to-night. Did you see, they have withdrawn the dragoons from the wood? They knew it would be of no use to keep them there. So now, good night—that's all settled."

"All settled, indeed," murmured Sir Robert Croyland as Mr. Radford left him; and for nearly half an hour after, he continued sitting in the library, with his hands clasped upon his knee, exactly in the same position.

CHAPTER VI.

Sir Edward Digby did not take advantage of the opportunity which Mrs. Barbara's absence afforded him. This may seem extraordinary conduct in a good soldier and quick and ready man; but he had his reasons for it. Not that he was beginning to hesitate, as some men do, when—after having quite made up their minds—they begin to consider all the perils of their situation, and retreat, without much regard for their own consistency, or the feelings of the other persons interested. But, no—Digby justly remembered that what he had to say might require some time, and that it might produce some agitation. Moreover, he recollected that there are few things so disagreeable on earth, as being interrupted at a time when people's eyes are sparkling or in tears, when the cheek is flushed or deadly pale; and as he knew not when Mrs. Barbara might return, and certainly did not anticipate that she would be long absent, he resolved to wait for another opportunity.

When he found minute after minute slip by, however, he began to repent of his determination; and certainly, although the word love never passed his lips, something very like the reality shone out in his eyes. Perhaps, had Zara been in any of her usual moods, more serious words might have followed. Had she been gay and jesting, or calm and thoughtful, a thousand little incidents might have led on naturally to the unfolding of the heart of each. But, on the contrary, she was neither the one nor the other. She was evidently anxious, apprehensive, ill at ease; and though she conversed rationally enough for a person whose mind was in such a state, yet she frequently turned her eyes towards the door of the adjoining room, from which the sound of her father's voice and that of Mr. Radford might still be heard.

Sir Edward Digby endeavoured to gain her attention to himself, as much with a view to withdraw it from unpleasant subjects as anything else; and it was very natural that—with one so fair and so excellent, one possessing so much brightness, in spite of a few little spots—it was natural that his tone should become tenderer every minute. At length, however, she stopped him, saying, "I am very anxious just now. I fear there is some mischief going on there, which we cannot prevent, and may never know. Edith's absence is certainly very strange; and I fear they may foil us yet."

In a minute or two after, Mrs. Barbara Croyland returned, but in such a flutter that she spoilt her embroidery, which she snatched up to cover her agitation, dropped her finest scissars, and broke the point off, and finally ran the needle into her finger, which, thereupon, spotted the silk with blood. She gave no explanation indeed of all this emotion, but looked several times at Zara with a meaning glance; and when, at length, Sir Robert Croyland entered the drawing room, his whole air and manner did not tend to remove from his daughter's mind the apprehension which his sister's demeanour had cast over it.

There is a general tone in every landscape which it never entirely loses; yet how infinite are the varieties which sunshine and cloud and storm, and morning, evening, and noon, bring upon it; and thus with the expression and conduct of every man, although they retain certain distinctive characteristics, yet innumerable are the varieties produced by the moods, the passions, and the emotions of the mind. Sir Robert Croyland was no longer irritably thoughtful; but he was stern, gloomy, melancholy. He strove to converse, indeed; but the effort was so apparent, the pain it gave him so evident, that Sir Edward Digby felt, or fancied, that his presence was a restraint. He had too much tact, however, to show that he imagined such to be the case; and he only resolved to retire to his own room as soon as he decently could. He was wrong in his supposition, indeed, that his host might wish to communicate something privately to Zara, or to Mrs. Barbara. Sir Robert had nothing to tell; and therefore the presence of Sir Edward Digby was rather agreeable to him than not, as shielding him from inquiries, which it might not have suited him to answer. He would have talked if he could, and would have done his best to make his house agreeable to his young guest; but his thoughts still turned, with all the bitterness of smothered anger, to the indignity he had suffered; and he asked himself, again and again, "Will the time ever come, when I shall have vengeance for all this?"

The evening passed gloomily, and in consequence slowly; and at length, when the clock showed that it still wanted a quarter to ten, Digby rose and bade the little party good night, saying that he was somewhat tired, and had letters to write.

"I shall go to bed too," said Sir Robert Croyland, ringing for his candle. But Digby quitted the room first; and Zara could not refrain from saying, in a low tone, as she took leave of her father for the night, and went out of the room with him, "There is nothing amiss with Edith, I trust, my dear father?"

"Oh dear, no!" answered Sir Robert Croyland, with as careless an air as he could assume. "Nothing at all, but that she does not come home to-night, and perhaps may not to-morrow."

Still unsatisfied, Zara sought her own room; and when her maid had half performed her usual functions for the night, she dismissed her, saying, that she would do the rest herself. When alone, however, Zara Croyland did not proceed to undress, but remained thinking over all the events of the day, with her head resting on her hand, and her eyes cast down. The idea of Edith and her fate mingled with other images.

The words that Digby had spoken, the increasing tenderness of his tone and manner, came back to memory, and made her heart flutter with sensations unknown till then. She felt alarmed at her own feelings; she knew not well what they were; but still she said to herself at every pause of thought—"It is all nonsense!—He will go away and forget me; and I shall forget him! These soldiers have always some tale of love for every woman's ear. It is their habit—almost their nature." Did she believe her own conclusions? Not entirely; but she tried to believe them; and that was enough for the present.

Some minutes after, however, when a light knock was heard at the door, she started almost as if some one had struck her; and Fancy, who is always drawing upon improbability, made her believe, for an instant, that it might be Digby. She said, "Come in," however, with tolerable calmness; and the next instant, the figure of her aunt presented itself, with eagerness in her looks and importance in her whole air.

"My dear child!" she said, "I did not know whether your maid was gone; but I am very happy she is, for I have something to tell you of very great importance indeed. What do you think that rascal Radford has done?" and as she spoke, she sank, with a dignified air, into a chair.

"I really can't tell, my dear aunt," replied Zara, not a little surprised to hear the bad epithet which her aunt applied to a gentleman, towards whom she usually displayed great politeness. "I am sure he is quite capable of anything that is bad."

"Ah, he is very much afraid of me, and what he calls my sweet meddling ways," said the old lady; "but, perhaps, if I had meddled before, it might have been all the better. I am sure I am the very last to meddle, except when there is an absolute occasion for it, as you well know, my dear Zara."

The last proposition was put in some degree as a question; but Zara did not think fit to answer it, merely saying, "What is it, my dear aunt?—I am all anxiety and fear regarding Edith."

"Well you may be, my love," said Mrs. Barbara; and thereupon she proceeded to tell Zara, how she had overheard the whole conversation between Mr. Radford and her brother, through the door of the library, which opened into the little passage, that ran between it and the rooms beyond. She did not say that she had put her ear to the keyhole; but that Zara took for granted, and indeed felt somewhat like an accomplice, while listening to secrets which had been acquired by such means.

Thus almost everything that had passed in the library—with a few very short variations and improvements, but with a good deal of comment, and a somewhat lengthy detail—was communicated by Mrs. Barbara to her niece; and when she had done, the old lady added, "There, my dear, now go to bed and sleep upon it; and we will talk it all over in the morning, for I am determined that my niece shall not be treated in such a way by any vagabond smuggler like that. Dear me! one cannot tell what might happen, with Edith shut up in his house in that way. Talk of my meddling, indeed! He shall find that I will meddle now to some purpose! Good night, my dear love—good night!" But Mrs. Barbara stopped at the door, to explain to Zara that she had not told her before, "Because, you know," said the good lady, "I could not speak of such things before a stranger, like Sir Edward Digby; and when he was gone, I didn't dare say anything to your father. Think of it till to-morrow, there's a dear girl, and try and devise some plan."

"I will," said Zara—"I will;" but as soon as her aunt had disappeared, she clasped her hands together, exclaiming, "Good Heaven! what plan can I form? Edith is lost! They have her now completely in their power. Oh, that I had known this before Sir Edward Digby went to sleep. He might have gone over to Leyton to-morrow, early; and they might have devised something together. Perhaps he has not gone to rest yet. He told me to throw off all restraint, to have no ceremony in case of need. Leyton told me so, too—that I might trust in him—that he is a man of honour. Oh, yes, I am sure he is a man of honour! but what will he think?—He promised he would think no harm of anything I might be called upon to do; and I promised I would trust him. I will go! He can speak to me in the passage. No one sleeps near, to overhear. But I will knock softly; for though he said he had letters to write, he may have gone to bed by this time."

Leaving the lights standing where they were, Zara cast on a long dressing-gown, and crept quietly out into the passage, taking care not to pull the door quite to. All was silent in the house; not a sound was heard; and with her heart beating as if it would have burst through her side, she approached Sir Edward Digby's door;—but there she paused. Had she not paused, but gone on at once, and knocked, all would have been well; for, so far from being in bed, he was sitting calmly reading. But ladies' resolutions, and men's, are made of very much the same materials. The instant her foot stopped, her whole host of woman's feelings crowded upon her, and barred the way. First, she thought of modesty, and propriety, and decency; and then, though she might have overcome the whole of that squadron for Edith's sake, the remembrance of many words that Digby had spoken, the look, the tone, the manner, all rose again upon her memory. She felt that he was a lover; and putting her hand to her brow, she murmured—"I cannot; no, I cannot. Had he been only a friend, I would.—I will see him early to-morrow. I will sit up all night, that I may not sleep, and miss the opportunity; but I cannot go to-night;" and, returning as quietly to her own chamber as she had come thence, she shut the door and locked it. She had never locked it in her life before; and she knew not why she did it.

Then, drawing the arm-chair to the hearth, Zara Croyland trimmed the fire, wrapped herself up as warmly as she could; and putting out one of the candles, that she might not be left in darkness by both being burnt out together, she took up a book, and began to read. From time to time, during that long night, her eyes grew heavy, and she fell asleep; but something always woke her. Either her own thoughts troubled her in dreams, or else the book fell out of her hand, or the wind shook the window, or the cold chill that precedes the coming morning disturbed her; and at length she looked at her watch, and, finding it past five o'clock, she congratulated herself at having escaped the power of the drowsy god, and, dressing in haste, undrew the curtains, and looked out by the light of the dawning day. When she saw the edge of the sun coming up, she said to herself, "He is often very early. I will go down." But, bethinking herself that no time was to be lost, she hurried first to her maid's room, and waking her, told her to see Sir Edward Digby's servant, as soon as he rose, and to bid him inform his master that she wanted to speak with him in the library. "Speak not a word of this to any one else, Eliza," she said; and then, thinking it necessary to assign some reason for her conduct, she added, "I am very anxious about my sister; her not coming home yesterday alarms me, and I want to hear more."

"Oh dear! you needn't frighten yourself, Miss Zara," replied the maid—"I dare say there's nothing the matter."

"But I cannot help frightening myself," replied Zara; and going down into the library, she unclosed one of the shutters.

The maid was very willing to gratify her young lady, for Zara was a favourite with all; but thinking from the look of the sky, that it would be a long time before the servant rose, and having no such scruples as her mistress, she went quietly away to his room, and knocked at his door, saying, "I wish you would get up, Mr. Somers—I want to speak with you."

Zara remained alone for twenty minutes in the library, or not much more, and then she heard Digby's step in the passage. There was a good deal of alarm and surprise in his look when he entered; but his fair companion's tale was soon told; and that sufficiently explained her sudden call for his presence. He made no comment at the moment, but replied, "Wait for me here one instant. I will order my horse, and be back directly."

He was speedily by her side again; and then, taking her hand in his, he said, "I wish I had known this, last night.—You need not have been afraid of disturbing me, for I was up till nearly one."

Zara smiled: "You do not know," she answered, "how near I was to your door, with the intention of calling you."

"And why did you not?" asked Digby, eagerly. "Nay, you must tell me, why you should hesitate when so much was at stake."

"I can but answer, because my heart failed me," replied Zara. "You know women's hearts are weak foolish things."

"Nay," said Digby, "you must explain further.—Why did your heart fail you? Tell me, Zara. I cannot rest satisfied unless you tell me."

"Indeed, there is no time now for explanation," she replied, feeling that her admission had drawn her into more than she had anticipated; "your horse will soon be here—and—and there is not a moment to lose."

"There is time enough for those who will," answered Digby, in a serious tone; "you promised me that you would not hesitate, whenever necessity required you to apply to me for counsel or aid — you have hesitated, Zara. Could you doubt me—could you be apprehensive—could you suppose that Edward Digby would, in word, deed, or thought, take advantage of your generous confidence?"

"No, no—oh, no!" answered Zara, warmly, blushing, and trembling at the same time, "I did not—I could not, after all you have done—after all I have seen. No, no; I thought you would think it strange—I thought——"

"Then you supposed I would wrong you in thought!" he replied, with some mortification in his manner; "you do not know me yet."

"Oh yes, indeed I do," she answered, feeling that she was getting further and further into difficulties; and then she added, with one of her sudden bursts of frankness, "I will tell you how it was—candidly and truly. Just as I was at your door, and about to knock, the memory of several things you had said—inadvertently, perhaps—crossed my mind; and, though I felt that I could go at any hour to consult a friend in such terrible circumstances, I could not—no, I could not do so with a—with one—You see what harm you have done by such fine speeches!"

She thought, that by her last words, she had guarded herself securely from any immediate consequences of this unreserved confession; but she was mistaken. She merely hurried on what might yet have rested for a day or two.

Sir Edward Digby took her other hand also, and held it gently yet firmly, as if he was afraid she should escape from him. "Zara," he said, "dear Zara, I have done harm, by speaking too much, or not enough. I must remedy it by the only means in my power.—Listen to me for one moment, for I cannot go till all is said. You must cast off this reserve—you must act perfectly freely with me; I seek to bind you by no engagement—I will bear my doubt; I will not construe anything you do, as an acceptance of my suit; but you must know—nay, you do know, you do feel, that I am your lover. It was doubt of your own sensations towards me, that made you hesitate—it was fear that you should commit yourself, to that which you might, on consideration, be indisposed to ratify.—You thought that I might plead such confidence as a tacit promise; and that made you pause. But hear me, as I pledge myself—upon my honour, as a gentleman—that if you act fearlessly and freely, in the cause in which we are both engaged—if you confide in me—trust in me, and never hesitate to put yourself, as you may think, entirely in my power, I will never look upon anything as plighting you to me in the slightest degree, till I hear you say the words, 'Digby, I am yours'—if ever that happy day should come. In the meantime, however, to set you entirely free from all apprehension of what others may say, I hold myself bound to you by every promise that man can make; and this very day I will ask your father's approbation of my suit. But I am well aware, though circumstances have shown me in a marvellous short time, that your heart and mind is equal to your beauty, yet it is not to be expected that such a being can be won in a few short days, and that I must wait in patience—not without hope, indeed, but with no presumption. By your conduct, at least, I shall know, whether I have gained your esteem.—Your love, perhaps, may follow; and now I leave you, to serve your sister and my friend, to the best of my power."

Thus saying, he raised her hand to his lips, kissed it, and moved towards the door.

There was a sad struggle in Zara's breast;

but as he was laying his hand upon the lock to open it, she said, "Digby—Digby—Edward!"

He instantly turned, and ran towards her; for her face had become very pale. She gave him her hand at once, however, "Kind, generous man!" she said, "you must not go without hearing my answer. Such a pledge cannot be all on one part. I am yours, Digby, if you wish it; yet know me better first before you answer—see all my faults, and all my failings. Even this must show you how strange a being I am—how unlike other girls—how unlike perhaps, the woman you would wish to call your wife!"

"Wish it!" answered Digby, casting his arm round her, "from my heart—from my very soul, Zara. I know enough, I have seen enough, for I have seen you in circumstances that bring forth the bosom's inmost feelings; and though you are unlike others—and I have watched many in their course—that very dissimilarity is to me the surpassing charm. They are all art, you are all nature—ay, and nature in its sweetest and most graceful form; and I can boldly say, I never yet saw woman whom I should desire to call my wife till I saw you. I will not wait, dear girl; but, pledged to you as you are pledged to me, will not press this subject further on you, till your sister's fate is sealed. I must, indeed, speak with your father at once, that there may be no mistake, no misapprehension; but till all this sad business is settled, we are brother and sister, Zara; and then a dearer bond."

"Oh, yes, yes—brother and sister!" cried Zara, clinging to him at a name which takes fear from woman's heart, "so will we be, Edward; and now all my doubts and hesitations will be at an end. I shall never fear more to seek you when it is needful."

"And my suit will be an excuse and a reason to all others, for free interviews, and solitary rambles, and private conference, and every dear communion," answered Digby, pleased, and yet almost amazed at the simplicity with which she lent herself to the magic of a word, when the heart led her.

But Zara saw he was a little extending the brother's privilege; and with a warm cheek but smiling lip, she answered, "There, leave me now; I see you are learned in the art of leading on from step to step. Go on your way, Edward; and, oh! be kind to me, and do not make me feel this new situation too deeply at first. There, pray take away your arm; none but a father's or a sister's has been there before; and it makes my heart beat, as if it were wrong."

But Digby kept it where it was for a moment or two longer, and gave a few instants to happiness, in which she shared, though it agitated her. "Nay, go," she said, at length, in a tone of entreaty, "and I will lie down and rest for an hour; for I have sat up all night by the fire, lest I should be too late.—You must go, indeed. There is your horse upon the terrace; and we must not be selfish, but remember poor Edith before we think of our own happiness."

There was a sweet and frank confession in her words that pleased Digby well; and leaving her with a heart at rest on his own account, he mounted his horse and rode rapidly away towards the quarters of Sir Henry Leyton.

CHAPTER VII

THE reader has doubtless remarked—for every reader who peruses a book to any purpose must remark everything, inasmuch as the most important events are so often connected with insignificant circumstances, that the one cannot be understood without the other—the reader has doubtless remarked, that Mr. Radford, on leaving Sir Robert Croyland, informed his unhappy victim, that he had still a good deal of business to do that night. Now, during the day he had—as may well be judged from his own statement of all the preparations he had already made—done a great deal of very important business; but the details of his past proceedings I shall not enter into, and only beg leave to precede him by a short time, to the scene of those farther operations which he had laid out as the close of that evening's labours. It is to the lone house, as it was called, near Iden Green, that I wish to conduct my companions, and a solitary and gloomy looking spot it was, at the time I speak of. All that part of the country is now very thickly inhabited: the ground bears nearly as large a population as it can support; and though there are still fields, and woods, and occasional waste places, yet no such events could now happen as those which occurred eighty or a hundred years ago, when one might travel miles, in various parts of Kent, without meeting a living soul. The pressure of a large population crushes out the bolder and more daring sorts of crime, and leaves small cunning to effect, in secret, what cannot be accomplished openly, under the police of innumerable eyes.

But it was not so in those days; and the lone house near Iden Green, whatever it was originally built for, had become the refuge and the lurking-place of some of the most fierce and lawless men in the country. It was a large building, with numerous rooms and passages; and it had stables behind it, but no walled court-yard; for the close sweeping round of the wood, a part of which still exists in great beauty, was a convenience on which its architect seemed to have calculated. Standing some way off the high road, and about half a mile from Collyer Green, it was so sheltered by trees that, on whichever side approached, nothing could be seen but the top of the roof and part of a garret-window, till one was within a short distance of the edifice. But that garret-window had its advantages; for it commanded a view over a great part of the country, on three sides, and especially gave a prospect of the roads in the neighbourhood.

The building was not a farm-house, for it had none of the requisites; it could not well be a public-house, though a sign swung before it; for the lower windows were boarded up, and the owner or tenant thereof, if any traveller whom he did not know, stopped at his door—which was, indeed, a rare occurrence—told him that it was all a mistake, and cursing the sign, vowed he would have it cut down. Nevertheless, if the Ramleys, or any of their gang, or, indeed, any members of a similar fraternity, came thither, the doors opened as if by magic; and good accommodation for man and horse was sure to be found within.

It was also remarked, that many a gentleman

n haste went in there, and was never seen to ssue forth again till he appeared in quite a different part of the country; and, had the master of the house lived two or three centuries earlier, he might on that very account have risked the fagot, on a charge of dealing with the devil. As t was, he was only suspected of being a coiner; out in regard to that charge, history has left no evidence, pro or con.

It was in this house, however, on the evening of the day subsequent to the discomfiture of the smugglers, that six men were assembled in a small room at the back, all of whom had, more or less, taken part in the struggle near Woodchurch. The two younger Ramleys were there, as well as one of the principal members of their gang, and two other men, who had been long engaged in carrying smuggled goods from the coast, as a regular profession; but who were, in other respects, much more respectable persons than those by whom they were surrounded. At the head of the table, however, was the most important personage of the whole: no other than Richard Radford himself, who had joined his comrades an hour or two before. The joy and excitement of his escape from the wood, the temporary triumph which he had obtained over the vigilance of the soldiery, and the effec produced upon a disposition naturally bold reckless, and daring, by the sudden chang from imminent peril to comparative security had all raised his spirits to an excessive pitch and, indeed, the whole party, instead of seeming depressed by their late disaster, appeared elevated with that wild and lawless mirth, which owns no tie or restraint, reverences nothing sacred or respectable. Spirits and water were circulating freely amongst them; and they were boasting of their feats in the late skirmish, or commenting upon its events, with many a jes and many a falsehood.

"The Major did very well, too," said Ned Ramley, "for he killed one of the dragoons, and wounded another, before he went down himself poor devil!"

"Here's to the Major's ghost!" cried young Radford, "and I'll try to give it satisfaction by avenging him. We'll have vengeance upon them yet, Ned."

"Ay, upon all who had any concern in it," answered Jim Ramley, with a meaning look.

"And first upon him who betrayed us," rejoined Richard Radford; "and I will have it, too in a way that shall punish him more than if we flogged him to death with horse-whips, as the

Sussex men did to Chater at the Flying Bull, near Hazlemere."

The elder of the two Ramleys gave a look towards the men who were at the bottom of the table; and Richard Radford, dropping his voice, whispered something to Ned Ramley, who replied aloud, with an oath, "I'd have taken my revenge, whatever came of it."

"No, no," answered Radford, "the red-coats were too near. However, all's not lost that's delayed. I wonder where that young devil, little Starlight's gone to. I sent him three hours ago to Cranbrook with the clothes, and told him to come back and tell me if she passed. She'll not go now, that's certain; for she would be in the dark. Have you any notion, Ned, how many men we could get together in case of need?"

"Oh, fifty or sixty!" said one of the men from the bottom of the table, who seemed inclined to have his share in the conversation, as soon as it turned upon subjects with which he was familiar; "there are seven or eight hid away down at Cranbrook, and nine or ten at Tenterden, with some of the goods, too."

"Ah, that's well!" answered young Radford; "I thought all the goods had been taken."

"Oh, dear no," replied Jim Ramley, "we've

got a thousand pounds' worth in this house and I dare say double as much is scatterec about in different hides. The light things wer got off; but they are the most valuable."

"I'll tell you what, my men," cried youn Radford, "as soon as these soldiers are gon down to the coast again, we'll all gather together and do some devilish high thing, just to shov them that they are not quite masters of th country yet. I've a great mind to burn thei inn at Woodchurch, just for harbouring them If we don't make these rascally fellows fear us the trade will be quite put down in the county.'

"I swear," exclaimed Ned Ramley, with a horrible blasphemy, "that if I can catch an one who has peached, even if it be but by on word, I will split his head like a lobster."

"And I, too!" answered his brother; anc several others joined in the oath.

The conversation then took another turn; anc while it went on generally around the table young Radford spoke several times in a lov voice to the two who sat next to him, and th name of Harding was more than once mentioned The glass circulated very freely also; and al though none of them became absolutely intoxi cated, yet all of them were more or less affecte by the spirits, when the boy, whom we have called Little Starlight, crept quietly into the room, and approached Mr. Radford.

"She's not come, sir," he said; "I waited a long while, and then went and asked the old woman of the shop, telling her that I was to be sure and see that Kate Clare got the bundle; but she said that she certainly wouldn't come to night."

"That's a good boy," said young Radford. "Go and tell the people to bring us some candles; and then I'll give you a glass of Hollands for your pains. It's getting infernally dark," he continued, "and as nothing more is to be done to-day, we may as well make a night of it."

"No, no," answered one of the men at the bottom of the table, "I've had enough, and I shall go and turn in."

Nobody opposed him; and he and his companion soon after left them. A smile passed round amongst the rest as soon as the two had shut the door.

"Now those puny fellows are gone," said Jim Ramley, "we can say what we like. First, let us talk about the goods, Mr. Radford, for I don't think they are quite safe here. They had better be got up to your father's as soon as possible, for if the house were to be searched, we could get out into the wood, but they could not."

"Hark!" said young Radford; "there's some one knocking hard at the house door, I think."

"Ay, trust all that to Obadiah," said Ned Ramley. "He wont open the door till he sees who it is."

The minute after, however, old Mr. Radford stood amongst them; and he took especial care not to throw any damp upon their spirits, but rather to encourage them, and make light of the late events. He sat down for a few minutes by his son, took a glass of Hollands and water, and then whispered to his hopeful heir that he wanted to speak with him for a minute. The young man instantly rose, and led the way out into the room opposite, which was vacant.

"By Heaven, Dick, this is an awkward job!" said his father; "the loss is enormous, and never to be recovered."

"The things are not all lost," answered Richard Radford. "A great quantity of the goods are about the country. There's a thousand pounds' worth, they say, in this house."

"We must have them got together as fast as possible," said Mr. Radford, "and brought up to our place. All that is here had better be sent up about three o'clock in the morning."

"I'll bring them up myself," replied his son.

"No, no, no!" said Mr. Radford; "you keep quiet where you are, till to-morrow night."

"Pooh, nonsense," answered the young man; "I'm not at all afraid.—Very well—very well, they shall come up, and I'll follow to-morrow night, if you think I can be at the Hall in safety."

"I don't intend you to be long at the Hall," answered Mr. Radford: "you must take a trip over the sea, my boy, till we can make sure of a pardon for you. There! you need not look so blank. You shan't go alone. Come up at eleven o'clock; and you will find Edith Croyland waiting to give you her hand, the next day.—Then a post-chaise and four, and a good tight boat on the beach, and you are landed in France in no time. Everything is ready—everything is settled; and with her fortune, you will have enough to live like a prince, till you can come back here."

All this intelligence did not seem to give Richard Radford as much satisfaction as his father expected. "I would rather have had little Zara, a devilish deal!" he replied.

"Very likely," answered his father, with his countenance changing, and his brow growing dark; "but that wont do, Dick. We have had enough nonsense of all sorts; and it must now be brought to an end. It's not the matter of the fortune alone; but I am determined that both you and I shall have revenge."

"Revenge!" said his son; "I don't see what revenge has to do with that."

"I'll tell you," answered old Mr. Radford, in a low tone, but bitter in its very lowness. "The man who so cunningly surrounded you and the rest yesterday morning, who took all my goods, and murdered many of our friends, is that very Harry Leyton, whom you've heard talk of. He has come down here on purpose to ruin you and me, if possible, and to marry Edith Croyland; but he shall never have her, by ——," and he added a fearful oath which I will not repeat.

"Ay, that alters the case," replied Richard Radford, with a demoniacal smile; "oh, I'll marry her and make her happy, as the people say. But I'll tell you what—I'll have my revenge, too, before I go, and upon one who is worse than the other fellow—I mean the man who betrayed us all."

"Who is that?" demanded the father.

"Harding," answered young Radford—"Harding."

"Are you sure that it was he?" asked the

old gentleman; "I have suspected him myself, but I have no proof."

"But I have," replied his son: "he was seen several nights before, by little Starlight, talking for a long while with this very Colonel of Dragoons, upon the cliff. Another man was with him, too—most likely Mowle; and then, again, yesterday evening, some of these good fellows who were on the look-out to help me, saw him speaking to a dragoon officer at Widow Clare's door; so he must be a traitor, or they would have taken him."

"Then he deserves to be shot," said old Radford, fiercely; "but take care, Dick: you had better not do it yourself. You'll find him difficult to get at, and may be caught."

"Leave him to me—leave him to me," answered his hopeful son; "I've a plan in my head that will punish him better than a bullet. But the bullet he shall have, too; for all the men have sworn that they will take his blood; but that can be done after I'm gone."

"But what's your plan, my boy?" asked old Mr. Radford.

"Never mind, never mind!" answered Richard, "I'll find means to execute it.—I only wish those dragoons were away from Harbourne Wood."

"Why, they are," exclaimed his father, laughing. "They were withdrawn this afternoon, and a party of them, too, marched out of Woodchurch, as if they were going to Ashford. I dare say, by this time to-morrow night, they will be all gone to their quarters again."

"Then it's all safe!" said his son; and after some more conversation between the two—and various injunctions upon the part of the old man, as to caution and prudence, upon the part of the young one, they parted for the time. Young Radford then rejoined his companions, and remained with them till about one o'clock in the morning, when the small portion of smuggled goods which had been saved, was sent off, escorted by two men, towards Radford Hall, where they arrived safely, and were received by servants well accustomed to such practices. They consisted of only one horse-load, indeed, so that the journey was quickly performed; and the two men returned before five. Although Richard Radford had given his father every assurance that he would remain quiet, and take every prudent step for his own concealment, his very first acts showed no disposition to keep his word. Before eight o'clock in the morning, he, the two Ramleys, and one or two other men, who had come in during the night, were out amongst the fields and woods, "reconnoitring," as they called it; but, with a spirit in their breasts, which rendered them ready for any rash and criminal act that might suggest itself. Thus occupied, I shall for the present leave them, and show more of their proceedings at a future period.

CHAPTER VIII.

Having now led the history of a great part of the personages in our drama up to the same point of time, namely, the third morning after the defeat of the smugglers, we may as well turn to follow out the course of Sir Edward Digby, on a day that was destined to be eventful to all the parties concerned. On arriving at Woodchurch, he found a small body of dragoons, ready mounted, at the door of the little inn, and two saddled horses, held waiting for their riders. Without ceremony, he entered, and went up at once to Leyton's room, where he found him, booted and spurred to set out, with Mowle the officer standing by him, looking on, while Sir Henry placed some papers in a writing-desk, and locked them up.

The young commander greeted his friend warmly; and then, turning to the officer of Customs, said, "If you will mount, Mr. Mowle, I will be down with you directly;" and as soon as Mowle, taking the hint, departed, he continued, in a quick tone, but with a faint smile upon his countenance, "I know your errand, Digby, before you tell it. Edith has been transferred to the good charge and guidance of Mr. Radford; but that has only prepared me to act more vigorously than ever. My scruples on Sir Robert Croyland's account are at an end.—Heaven and earth! Is it possible that a man can be so criminally weak, as to give his child up—a sweet, gentle girl like that—to the charge of such a base unprincipled scoundrel!"

"Nay, nay, we must do Sir Robert justice," answered Digby. "It was done without his consent—indeed, against his will; and, a more impudent and shameless piece of trickery was never practised. You must listen for one moment, Leyton, though you seem in haste;" and he proceeded to detail to him, as succinctly as possible, all that had occurred between Mr. Radford and Edith's father on the preceding evening, stating his authority, and whence Zara had received her information."

"That somewhat alters the case, indeed;" answered Leyton; "but it must not alter my conduct. I am, indeed, in haste, Digby, for I hope, ere two or three hours are over, to send the young scoundrel, for whose sake all this is done, a prisoner to the gaol. Mowle has somehow got information of where he is—from undoubted authority, he says; and we are away to Iden Green, in consequence. We shall get more information by the way; and I go with the party for a certain distance, in order to be at hand, in case of need; but, as it does not do for me, in my position, to take upon me the capture of half-a-dozen smugglers, the command of the party will rest with Cornet Joyce. We will deal with Mr. Radford, the father, afterwards. But, in the meantime, Digby, as your information certainly gives a different view of the case, from that which I had before taken, you will greatly oblige me if you can contrive to ride over to Mr. Croyland's, and see if you can find Mr. Warde there. Beg him to let me have the directions he promised, by four o'clock to-day; and if you do not find him, leave word to that effect, with Mr. Croyland himself."

"You seem to place great faith in Warde," said Sir Edward Digby, shaking his head.

"I have cause—I have cause, Digby," answered his friend. "But I must go, lest this youth escape me again."

"Well, God speed you, then," replied Digby. "I will go to Mr. Croyland at once, and can contrive, I dare say, to get back to Harbourne by breakfast time. It is not above two or three miles round, and I will go twenty, at any time, to serve you, Leyton."

Sir Edward Digby found good Mr. Zachary Croyland walking about in his garden, in a state of irritation indescribable. He, also, was aware, by this time, of what had befallen his niece; and such was his indignation, that he could scarcely find it in his heart to be even commonly civil to any one. On Sir Edward Digby delivering his message, as he found that Mr. Warde was not there, the old gentleman burst forth, exclaiming, "What have I to do with Warde, sir, or your friend either, sir?—Your friend's a fool! He might have walked out of that door with Edith Croyland in his hand; and that's no light prize, let me tell you; but he chose to be delicate, and gentlemanly, and all that sort of stupidity, and you see what has come of it. And now, forsooth, he sends over to ask advice and directions from Warde.

Well, I will tell the man, if I see him—thoug Heaven only knows whether that will be th case or not."

"Sir Henry Leyton seems to place great con fidence in Mr. Warde," replied Digby, "which trust may be justified."

Mr. Croyland looked at him sharply, for moment, from under his cocked hat, and then ex claimed, "Pish! you are a fool, young man.— There, don't look so fierce. I've given over fight ing for these twenty years; and, besides—yo wouldn't come to the duello with little Zara' uncle, would you? Ha, ha, ha!—Ha, ha, ha!— Ha, ha, ha!" and he laughed immoderately, bu splenetically enough at the same time. "But ought to have put my meaning as a question, no as a proposition," he continued. "Are yo such a fool as not to know the difference be tween an odd man and a madman, an eccentri man and a lunatic? If so, you had better ge away as fast as possible; for you and I ar likely soon to fall out. I understand wha you mean about Warde, quite well; but can tell you, that if you think Warde mad I'm quite as mad as he is, only that hi oddities lie all on the side of goodness an philanthropy, and mine now and then tak a different course. But get you gone—get you gone; you are better than the rest of them, I believe. I do hope and trust you'll marry Zara; and then you'll plague each other's souls, to my heart's content."

He held his hand out as he spoke; and Digby shook it, laughing good-humouredly; but, ere he had taken ten steps towards the door of the house, through which he had to pass before he could mount his horse, Mr. Croyland called after him, "Digby, Digby!—Sir Eddard!—Eldest son! I say,—how could you be such a fool as not to run that fellow through the stomach when you had him at your feet? You see what a quantity of mischief has come of it. You are all fools together, you soldiers, I think;—but it's true, a fool does as well as anything else to be shot at. —How's your shoulder? Better, I suppose."

"I have not thought of it for the last two days," replied Digby.

"Well, that will do," said Mr. Croyland. "Cured by the first intention. There, you may go: I don't want you. Only, pray tell my brother, that I think him as great a rascal as old Radford.—He'll know how much that means.—One's a weak rascal, and the other's a strong one; that's the only difference between them;

and Robert may fit on which cap he like best."

Digby did not think it necessary to stop t justify Sir Robert Croyland in his brother' opinion; but, mounting his horse, he rode bac across the country towards Harbourne as fas as he could go. He reached the house be fore the usual breakfast hour; but he found tha everybody there had been an early riser as wel as himself; the table was laid ready for breakfast and Sir Robert Croyland was waiting in the draw ing-room with some impatience in his looks.

"I think I am not too late, Sir Robert," sai Digby, taking out his watch, and bowing with smile to Zara and Mrs. Barbara.

"No, oh dear, no, my young friend," replie the baronet; "only in such a house as this breakfast is going on all the morning long; an I thought you would excuse me, if I took min a little earlier than usual, as I have got som way to go this morning."

This was said as they were entering th breakfast-room; but Sir Edward Digby replied promptly, "I must ask you to spare me fiv minutes before you go, Sir Robert, as I wisl to speak with you for a short time."

His host looked uneasy; for he was in tha

nervous and agitated state of mind, in which anything that is not clear and distinct seems terrible to the imagination, from the consciousness that many ill-defined calamities are hanging over us. He said, "Certainly, certainly!" however, in a polite tone; but he swallowed his breakfast in haste; and the young officer perceived that his host looked at every mouthful he took, as if likely to procrastinate the meal. Zara's face, too, was anxious and thoughtful; and consequently he hurried his own breakfast as fast as possible, knowing that the signal to rise would be a relief to all parties.

"If you will come into my little room, Sir Edward," said the master of the house, as soon as he saw that his guest was ready, "I shall be very happy to hear what you have to say."

Sir Edward Digby followed in silence; and, to tell the truth, his heart beat a good deal, though it was not one to yield upon slight occasions.

"I will not detain you a moment, Sir Robert," he said, when they had entered, and the door was shut, "for what I have to say will be easily answered. I am sensible, that yesterday my attention to your youngest daughter must have been remarked by you, and, indeed, my manner altogether must have shown you, and herself also, that I feel differently towards her and other women. I do not think it would be right to continue such conduct for one moment longer, without your approbation of my suit; and I can only further say, that if you grant me your sanction, I feel that I can love her deeply and well, that I will try to make her happy to the best of my power, and that my fortune is amply sufficient to maintain her in the station of life in which she has always moved, and to make such a settlement upon her as I trust will be satisfactory to you. I will not detain you to expatiate upon my feelings; but such is a soldier's straightforward declaration, and I trust you will countenance and approve of my addressing her."

Sir Robert Croyland shook him warmly by the hand. "My dear Sir Edward," he said, 'you are your father's own son—frank, candid, and honourable. He was one of the most gentlemanly and amiable men I ever knew; and it will give me heartfelt pleasure to see my dear child united to his son. But—indeed, I must deal with you as candidly——" He hesitated for a moment or two, and then went on—"Perhaps you think that circumstances here are more favourable than they really are. Things may come to your knowledge—things may have to be related—Zara's fortune will be——"

Sir Edward Digby saw that Sir Robert Croyland was greatly embarrassed; and for an instant—for love is a very irritable sort of state, at least for the imagination, and he was getting over head and ears in love, notwithstanding all his good resolutions—for an instant, I say, he might think that Zara had been engaged before, and that Sir Robert was about to tell him, that it was not the ever-coveted, first freshness of the heart he was to possess in her love, even if it were gained entirely. But a moment's thought, in regard to her father's situation, together with the baronet's last words, dispelled that unpleasant vision, and he replied, eagerly, "Oh, my dear sir, that can make no difference in my estimation. If I can obtain her full and entire love, no external circumstance whatsoever can at all affect my views.—I only desire her hand."

"No external circumstances whatsoever!" said Sir Robert Croyland, pausing on the words. "Are you sure of your own firmness, Sir Edward Digby? If her father were to tell you he is a ruined man—if he had many circumstances to relate which might make it painful to you to connect yourself with him—I do not say that it is so; but if it were?"

"Rather an awkward position!" thought Sir Edward Digby; but his mind was fully made up; and he replied, without hesitation, "It would still make no difference in my eyes, Sir Robert. I trust that none of these terrible things are the case, for your sake; but I should despise myself, if, with enough of my own, I made fortune any ingredient in my considerations, or if I could suffer my love for a being perfectly amiable in herself, to be affected by the circumstances of her family."

Sir Robert Croyland wrung his hand hard; and Digby felt that it was a sort of compact between them. "I fear I must go," said Zara's father, "and therefore I cannot explain more; but it is absolutely necessary to tell you that all my unmortgaged property is entailed, and will go to my brother, that Edith's fortune is totally independent, and that Zara has but a tithe of what her sister has."

"Still I say, as I said before," replied Digby, "that nothing of that kind can make any difference to me; nor will I ever suffer any consideration, not affecting your daughter personally—and I beg this may be clearly understood—to make any change in my views. If I can win her love—her entire, full, hearty love—with your sanction, she is mine. Have I that sanction, Sir Robert?"

"Fully, and from my heart," replied Sir Robert Croyland, with the unwonted tears coursing over his cheeks. "Go to her, my dear friend—go to her, and make what progress you may, with my best wishes. This is indeed a great happiness—a great relief!"

Thus saying, he followed Sir Edward Digby out of the room; and, mounting a new horse which had been brought up from his bailiff's, he rode slowly and thoughtfully away. As he went, a faint hope—nay, it could hardly be called a hope—a vague, wild fancy of explaining his whole situation to Sir Edward Digby, and gaining the blessed relief of confidence and counsel, arose in Sir Robert Croyland's breast.

Alas! what an unhappy state has been brought about by the long accumulation of sin and deceit which has gathered over human society! that no man can trust another fully! that we dare not confide our inmost thoughts to any! that there should be a fear—the necessity for a fear—of showing the unguarded heart to the near and dear! that every man should—according to the most accursed axiom of a corrupt world—live with his friend as if he were one day to be his enemy. Oh, truth, and honour, and sincerity! oh, true Christianity! whither are ye gone? Timidity soon banished such thoughts from the breast of Sir Robert Croyland, though there was something in the whole demeanour of his daughter's lover which showed him that, if ever man was to be trusted, he might trust there; and had he known how deeply Digby was already acquainted with much that concerned him, he might perhaps have gone one step farther, and told him all. As it was, he rode on, and soon gave himself up to bitter thoughts again.

In the meantime, Sir Edward Digby returned to Zara and Mrs. Barbara in the drawing-room, with so well satisfied a look, that it was evident to both, his conversation with Sir Robert had not referred to any unpleasant subject, and had not had any unpleasant result. He excited the elder lady's surprise, however, and produced some slight agitation in the younger, by taking Zara by the hand, and in good set terms of almost formal courtesy, requesting a few minutes' private audience. Her varying colour, and her hesitating look, showed her lover that she apprehended something more unpleasant than he had to say; and he whispered, as they went along towards the library, "It is nothing—it is nothing but to tell you what I have done, and to arrange our plan of campaign."

Zara looked up in his face with a glad smile, as if his words took some terror from her heart; and as soon as he was in the room, he let go her hand, and turned the key in such a manner in the door, that the key-hole could not serve the purpose of a perspective glass, even if it might that of an ear-trumpet.

"Forgive me, dear Zara," he said, "if I take care to secure our defences; otherwise, as your good aunt is perfectly certain that I am about to fall on my knees, and make my declaration, she might be seized with a desire to witness the scene, not at all aware that it has been performed already. But not to say more," he continued, "on a subject on which you have kindly and frankly set a lover's heart at rest, let me only tell you that your father has fully sanctioned my suit, which I know, after what you have said, will not be painful to you to hear."

"I was sure he would," answered Zara;

"not that he entered into any of my aunt's castles in the air, or that he devised my schemes, Digby; but, doubtless, he wishes to see a fortuneless girl well married, and would have been content with a lover for her, who might not have suited herself quite so well. You see I deal frankly with you, Digby, still; and will do so both now and hereafter, if you do not check me."

"Never, never will I!" answered Sir Edward Digby; "it was so you first commanded my esteem, even before my love; and so you will always keep it."

"Before your love?" said Zara, in an unwontedly serious tone; "your love is very young yet, Digby; and sometimes I can hardly believe all this to be real.—Will it last? or will it vanish away like a dream, and leave me waking, alone and sorrowful?"

"And yours for me, Zara?" asked her lover; but then, he added, quickly, "no, I will not put an unfair question: and every question is unfair that is already answered in one's own heart. Yours will, I trust, remain firm for me—so mine, I know, will for you, because we have seen each other under circumstances which have called forth the feelings, and displayed fully all the inmost thoughts which years of ordinary intercourse might not develop. But now, dear Zara, let us speak of our demeanour to each other. It will, perhaps, give us greater advantage if you treat me—perhaps, as a favoured, but not yet as an accepted lover. I will appear willingly as your humble slave and follower, if you will, now and then, let me know in private that I am something dearer; and by keeping up the character with me, which has gained you your uncle's commendation as a fair coquette, you may, perhaps, reconcile Mrs Barbara to many things, which her notions of propriety might interfere with, if they were done as between the betrothed."

"I fear I shall manage it but badly, Digby," she answered. "It was very easy to play the coquette before, when no deeper feelings were engaged, when I cared for no one, when all were indifferent to me. It might be natural to me, then; but I do not think I could play the coquette with the man I loved. At all events, I should act the part but badly, and should fancy he was always laughing at me in his heart, and triumphing over poor Zara Croyland, when he knew right well that he had the strings of the puppet in his hand. However, I will do my best, if you wish it; and I do believe, from knowing more of this house than you do, that your plan is a good one. The airs I have given myself, and the freedom I have taken, have been of service both to myself and Edith—to her in many ways, and to myself in keeping from me all serious addresses from men I could not love.—Yours is the first proposal I have ever had, Digby; so do not let what my uncle has said, make you believe that you have conquered a queen of hearts, who has set all others at defiance."

"No *gentleman* was ever refused by a *lady*," answered Digby, laying a strong emphasis on each noun-substantive.

"So, then, you were quite sure, before you said a word!" cried Zara, laughing. "Well, that is as frank a confession as any of my own! And yet you might have been mistaken; for esteeming you as I did, and circumstanced as I was, I would have trusted you as much, Digby, if you had been merely a friend."

"But you would not have shown me the deeper feelings of your heart upon other indifferent subjects," replied her lover.

Zara blushed, and looked down; then suddenly changed the course of conversation, saying, "But you have not told me what Leyton thought of all this, and what plans you have formed. What is to be done? Was he not deeply grieved and shocked?"

Sir Edward Digby told her all that had passed, and then added, "I intend now to send out my servant, Somers, to reconnoitre. He shall waylay Leyton on his return, and bring me news of his success. If this youth be safely lodged in gaol, his pretensions are at an end, at least for the present; but if he again escape, I think, ere noon to-morrow, I must interfere myself. I have now a better right to do so than I have hitherto had; and what I have heard from other quarters will enable me to speak boldly—even to your father, dear one—without committing either you or Edith."

Zara paused and thought; but all was still dark on every side, and she could extract no ray of light from the gloom. Digby did not fail (as, how could a lover neglect?) to try to lead her mind to pleasanter themes; and he did so in some degree. But we have been too long eaves-dropping upon private intercourse, and we will do so no more. The rest of the day passed in that mingled light and shade, which has a finer interest than the mere broad sunshine, till the return of Sir Robert Croyland, when the deep sadness that overspread his countenance clouded the happiness of all the rest.

Shortly after, Zara saw her lover's servant ride up the road, at considerable speed; and as it wanted but half-an-hour to dinner-time, Digby, who marked his coming also, retired to dress. When he returned to the drawing-room, there was a deeper and a sterner gloom upon his brow than the fair girl had ever seen; but her father and aunt were both present, and no explanation could take place. After dinner, too, Sir Robert Croyland and his guest returned to the drawing-room together; and though the cloud was still upon Digby's countenance, and he was graver than he had ever before appeared, yet she whom he loved could gain no tidings. To her he was still all tenderness and attention; but Zara could not play the part she had undertaken; and often her eyes rested on his face, with a mute, sad questioning, which made her aunt say to herself, "Well, Zara is in love at last!"

Thus passed a couple of hours, during which not above ten words were uttered by Sir Robert Croyland. At length, lights were brought in, after they had been for some time necessary; and at the end of about ten minutes more, the sound of several horses coming at a quick pace was heard. The feet stopped at the great door, the bell rang, and voices sounded in the hall. The tones of one, deep, clear, and mellow, made both Zara and her father start; and in a minute after, the butler entered—he was an old servant—saying, in a somewhat embarrassed manner, "Colonel Sir Henry Leyton, sir, wishes to speak with you immediately on business of importance."

"Who—who?" demanded Sir Robert, "Sir Henry Leyton!—Well, well, take him in somewhere!"

He rose from his chair, but staggered perceptibly for a moment; then, overcoming the emotion that he could not but feel, he steadied himself by the arm of his chair, and left the room. Zara gazed at Digby, and he at her he loved; but this night Mrs. Barbara thought fit to sit where she was; and Digby, approaching Zara's seat, bent over her, whispering, "Leyton has a terrible tale to tell; but not affecting Edith. She is safe.—What more he seeks, I do not know."

CHAPTER IX.

After parting with Sir Edward Digby at Woodchurch, Henry Leyton had ridden on at a quick pace to Park-gate, and thence along the high road, to Cranbrook. He himself was habited in the undress of his regiment, though with pistols at his saddle, and a heavy sword by his side. One of his servants followed him similarly accoutred, and an orderly accompanied the servant, while by the young officer's side appeared our good friend Mr. Mowle, heavily armed, with the somewhat anomalous equipments of a riding officer of Customs in those days. At a little distance behind this first group, came Cornet Joyce, and his party of dragoons; and in this order they all passed through Cranbrook, about nine o'clock; but a quarter of a mile beyond the little town they halted, and Mowle rode on for a short way alone, to the edge of Hangley Wood, which was now close before them. There he dismounted, and went in amongst the trees; but he was not long absent, for in less than five minutes he was by the colonel's side again. "All's right, sir," he said, "the boy assures me that they were all there still, at six this morning, and that their captain, Radford, does not move till after dark, to-night. So now we shall have the worst fellows amongst them—the two Ramleys and all."

"Well, then," answered Leyton, "you had better go on at once with the party, keeping through the wood. I will remain behind, coming on slowly; and if wanted, you will find me somewhere in the Hanger. Cornet Joyce has his orders in regard to surrounding the house; but of course he must act according to circumstances."

No more words were needed: the party of dragoons moved on rapidly, with Mowle at their head; and Leyton, after pausing for a few minutes on the road, dismounted, and giving his rein to the servant, walked slowly on into the wood, telling the two men who accompanied him, to follow. There was, at that time, as there is now, I believe, a broad road through Hangley Wood, leading into the cross-road from Biddenden to Goudhurst; but at that period, instead of being tolerably straight and good, it was very tortuous, rough, and uneven. Along this forest path, for so it might be called, the dragoons had taken their way, at a quick trot; and by it their young colonel followed, with his arms crossed upon his chest, and his head bent down, in deep and anxious meditation. The distance across the wood at that part is nearly a mile; and when he had reached the other side, Leyton turned upon his steps again, passed his servant and the orderly, and walked slowly on the road back to Cranbrook. The two men went to the extreme verge of the wood, and looked out towards Iden Green for a minute or two before they followed their officer, so that in the turnings of the road, they were out of sight by the time he had gone a quarter of a mile.

Leyton's thoughts were busy, as may be well supposed; but at length they were suddenly interrupted by loud, repeated, and piercing shrieks, apparently proceeding from a spot at some distance before him. Darting on, with a single glance behind, and a loud shout to call the men up, he rushed forward along the road, and the next instant beheld a sight which made his blood boil with indignation. At first, he merely perceived a girl, struggling in the hands of some five or six ruffians, who were maltreating her in the most brutal manner; but in another instant, as, drawing his sword, he rushed forward, he recognised—for it can scarcely be said, he saw—poor Kate Clare. With another loud shout to his men to come up, he darted on without pause or hesitation; but his approach was observed—the ruffians withdrew from around their victim; and one of them exclaimed, "Run, run! the dragoons are coming!"

"D— me! give her a shot before you go," cried another, "or she'll peach."

"Let her," cried young Radford—"but here goes;" and, turning as he hurried away, he deliberately fired a pistol at the unhappy girl, who was starting up wildly from the ground. She instantly reeled and fell, some seconds before Leyton could reach her; for he was still at the distance of a hundred yards.

All this had taken place in an inconceivably short space of time; but the next minute, the panic with which the villains had been seized subsided a little. One turned to look back—another turned—they beheld but one man on the road; and all the party were pausing, when

Leyton reached poor Kate Clare, and raised her in his arms. It might have fared ill with him had he been alone; but just at that moment the orderly appeared at the turn, coming up at the gallop, with the young officer's servant behind him; and not doubting that a large party was following, Radford and his companions fled as fast as they could.

"On after them, like lightning!" cried Leyton, as the men came up. "Leave the horse, leave the horse, and away! Watch them wherever they go, especially the man in the green coat! Take him if you can—shoot him dead if he resist. Ah, my poor girl!" he cried, with the tears rising in his eyes, "this is sad, indeed!—Where has he wounded you?"

"There," said Kate, faintly, taking away her hand, which was pressed upon her right side; "but that was his kindest act.—Thank God, I am dying!"

"Nay, nay," answered Leyton, "I trust not!" But the blood poured rapidly out, staining all her dress, which was torn and in wild disorder, and so rapidly did it flow, that Leyton clearly saw her words would probably prove too true. "Who was that villain?" he cried; "I will punish him if there be justice on earth!"

"Don't you know him?" said Kate, her voice growing more and more low. "I thought you were seeking him—Richard Radford."

"The atrocious scoundrel!" said Leyton; and drawing his handkerchief from his breast, he tied it tightly over her side, trying, though he saw it was nearly in vain, to stanch the blood, while at the same time he supported her against his knee with one arm thrown round her waist. Poor Kate closed her eyes with a faint shudder; and for a moment Leyton thought she was dead. She appeared to be reviving again, however, when a loud voice, not far distant, exclaimed, "Ha,—halloo! What the devil is this?"

Leyton looked suddenly up—for his eyes had been bent upon the poor girl's face for several minutes—and then beheld, hurrying up the road with a look of fury in his countenance, Kate's promised husband, Harding. With a violent oath the man rushed on, exclaiming, "Kate, what is all this?—Villain, have you misused the girl?"

"Hush, hush!" cried Leyton, with a stern gesture of his hand; "she is dying!—I would have saved her if I could; but alas, I came too late!"

The whole expression of Harding's countenance changed in an instant. Grief and terror succeeded to rage ; and, catching her franticly in his arms, he exclaimed—" Kate, Kate, speak to me !—Tell me, who has done this ?"

" I can tell you," answered Leyton—" Richard Radford."

While he was speaking, Kate Clare opened her eyes again, and gazed on Harding's face, moving her right hand faintly round and placing it upon his.

" Give me that handkerchief from your neck," said Leyton ; " if we can stop the blood, we may save her, yet. I have seen very bad wounds recovered from——"

" No, no !" said Kate Clare ; " thank God, I am dying—I would rather die !—Harding, I am not in fault—they caught me in the wood—oh, they treated me horribly. Mr. Radford said it was revenge—God forgive him, God forgive him ! But I would rather die thus in your arms —do not try to stop it—it is all in vain."

Leyton and Harding still persisted, however, and bound another handkerchief tight over the wound, in some degree diminishing the stream of blood, but yet, not stopping it entirely.

" Let us carry her to some house," cried Leyton, " and then send for assistance. See ! her lips are not so pale."

"I will carry her," cried Harding, raising her in his powerful arms.

"To my aunt's, then—to my aunt's, Harding," murmured Kate; "I would sooner die there than in any other place." And on Harding sped, without reply, while Leyton, sheathing his sword, which he had cast down, followed him, inquiring, "Is it far?"

"But a step, sir," answered the smuggler. "Pray, come with us.—This must be avenged."

"It shall," replied Leyton, sternly; "but I must stay here for a minute or two, till you can send somebody to me, to take my place, and let my men know where I am when they return."

Harding nodded his head, and then turned his eyes upon the face of the poor girl whom he bore in his arms, hurrying on without a moment's pause, till he was lost to the young officer's sight.

It is needless to describe the feelings of a high-minded and noble man like Leyton, when left alone to meditate over the horrible outrage which had been committed under his very eyes. He gave way to no burst of indignation, indeed, but with a frowning brow walked back upon the road, caught his horse without difficulty, and mounting, remained fixed near the spot where poor Kate had received her death-wound, like a soldier upon guard. In less than ten minutes, a lad ran up, saying, "Mr. Harding sent me, sir."

"Well, then, walk up and down here, my good boy," replied Leyton, "till some one comes to inquire for me. If it should be a servant, or a single soldier, send him down to the place which you came from, and wait where you are till a larger party of dragoons come up, when you must tell them the same—to go down to me there. If the party come first, wait for the servant and the soldier."

Having given these directions, he was turning away, but paused again to inquire his way to the place where Harding was; and then pointing to a bundle that lay upon the road, he said—"You had better bring that with you."

Following the boy's direction, as soon as he issued out of the wood, Sir Henry Leyton turned through a little field to the left; and seeing a small farm-house at some distance before him, he leaped his horse over two fences to abridge the way. Then riding into the farm-yard, he sprang to the ground, looking round for some one to take his charger. Several men of different ages were running about with eagerness and haste in their faces. Horses were being led forth from the stable; guns were in the hands of several; and one of them—a fine, tall, powerful young fellow—exclaimed, as soon as he saw Leyton—"We will catch them, sir—we will catch them! and by —— they shall be hanged as high as Haman for hurting the poor dear girl ——. Here, take his honour's horse, Bill."

"Is she still living?" asked Leyton.

"Oh dear, yes, sir!" cried the young man; "she seemed somewhat better for what mother gave her."

"Well, then," rejoined the young officer, "if you are going to search for these scoundrels, gallop up to the wood as fast as you can; you will find my servant and a trooper watching. They will give you information of which way the villains are gone. I will join you in a minute or two with a stronger force."

"Oh, sir, we shall do—we shall do," cried William Harris; "we will raise the whole county as we go, and will hunt them down like foxes. Do they think that our sisters and our wives are to be ill-used and murdered by such scum as they are?" and at the same time he sprang upon his horse's back. Leyton turned towards the house, but met the old farmer himself coming out with a great cavalry sword in his hand, and the butt end of a pistol sticking out of each pocket. "Quick, quick! to your horses!" he cried, "they shall rue the day—they shall rue the day!—Ah, sir, go in," he continued, seeing Leyton; "she is telling my wife and Harding all about it; but I can't stop to hear.—I will have that young Radford's blood, if I have a soul to be saved!"

"Better take him alive, and hand him over to justice," said Leyton, going into the house.

"D——n him, I'll kill him like a dog!" cried the farmer; and mounting somewhat less nimbly than his son, he put himself at the head of the whole party assembled, and rode fast away towards Hangley Wood.

In the meantime, Leyton entered the kitchen of the farm; but it was quite vacant. Voices, however, were heard speaking above, and he ventured to go up and enter the room. Three or four women were assembled there round good Mrs. Harris's own bed, on which poor Kate Clare was stretched, with Harding on his knees beside her, and her hand in his, the hot tears of man's bitterest agony, coursing each other down his bronzed and weather-beaten cheek.

"There, there!" said Mrs. Harris; "don't take on so, Harding—you only keep down her spirits. She might do very well, if she would but take heart. You see she is better for the cordial stuff I gave her."

Harding made no reply; but Kate Clare faintly shook her head; and Leyton, after having gazed on the sad scene for a moment, with bitter grief and indignation in his heart, drew back, thinking that his presence would only be a restraint to Kate's family and friends. He made a sign, however, to one of the women before he went, who followed him out of the room.

"I merely wish to tell you," he said, in a low voice, when the woman joined him at the top of the stairs, "that I am going back to the wood, to aid in the pursuit of these villains; for I can be of no use here, and may be there. If any of my people come, tell them where to find me; bid them follow me instantly, and stop every man on foot they see quitting the wood, till he gives an account of himself.—But had you not better send for a surgeon?"

"One is sent for, sir," replied the woman; "but I think she is not so bad as she was.—I'll take care and tell your people. I do hope they will catch them, for this is *too* bad."

Without more words Leyton went down, remounted his horse, and galloped back towards the edge of the wood. The news of what had happened, however, seemed to have spread over the country with the speed of lightning; for he saw four or five of the peasantry on horseback, already riding in the same direction across the fields. Two stout farmers joined him as he went, and both were already full of the story of poor Kate Clare. Rage and indignation were universal amongst the people; but as usual on such occasions, one proposed one plan, and another the other, so that by want of combination in their operations, all their resolution and eagerness were likely to be fruitlessly employed.

Leyton knew that it was of little use to argue on such points with undisciplined men; and his only trust was in the speedy arrival of the soldiers from Iden Green. When he reached the edge of the wood, however, with his two companions, they came upon farmer Harris's party, now swelled to twelve or thirteen men; and at the same moment his own servant rode round, exclaiming, as soon as he saw his master, "They are still in the wood, sir, if they have not come out this way. They dispersed so that we could not follow them on horseback, and we galloped out by different ways to watch."

"They haven't come here," cried Farmer Harris, "or we should have seen them. So now we have them safe enough."

"Ride off towards Iden Green," said Leyton to the servant, "and direct Cornet Joyce to bring down his men at the gallop to the edge of the copse. Let him dismount twelve on the north side of the wood, and, with all the farm-servants and country people he can collect, sweep it down, while the rest of the mounted men advance, on a line, on either side.—Stay, I will write;" and tearing a leaf out of his pocket-book, he put down his orders in pencil.

The man had just galloped away, when the young farmer, William Harris, shouted, "There they go—there they go! After them!—after them! Tally ho!" and instantly set spurs to his horse. All the rest but Leyton followed at full speed; but he paused, and, directing his eyes along the edge of the wood, clearly saw, at the distance of somewhat more than half a mile, three men, who seemed to have issued forth from amongst the trees, running across the fields as fast as they could go. It would seem that they had not been aware of the numbers collected to intercept them, till they had advanced too far to retreat; but they had got a good start; the country was difficult for any but well-trained horses; and darting on, they took their way towards Goudhurst, passing within a hundred yards of the spot where the victim of their horrid barbarity lay upon the bed of death.

Taking the narrow paths, leaping the stiles and gates, they at first seemed to gain upon the mass of peasantry who followed them, though their pursuers were on horseback and they on foot. But, well knowing the country, the farmers spread out along the small bridle-roads; and, while the better mounted horsemen followed direct across the fields, the others prepared to cut off the ruffians on the right and left. Gradually a semi-circle, enclosing them within its horns, was thus formed; and all chance of escape by flight was thus cut off.

In this dilemma, the three miscreants made straight towards a farm-house at which they occasionally received hospitality in their lawless expeditions, and which bears the name of "Smuggler Farm" to this day; but they knew not that all hearts had been raised against them by their late atrocities, and that the very tenant of the farm himself was now one of the foremost in pursuit. Rushing in, then, with no farther ceremony than casting the door open, they locked and barred it, just as some of the peasantry were closing in upon them; and then, hurrying to the kitchen, where the farmer's wife, his sister, and a servant was collected, Ned Ramley, who was the first, exclaimed, "Have you no hide, good dame?"

"Hide!" replied the stout farmer's wife, eyeing him askance—"not for such villains as you! Give me the spit, Madge; I've a great mind to run him through." Ned Ramley drew a pistol from his pocket; but at that moment the window was thrown up, the back door of the house was cast open, and half-a-dozen of the stout yeomanry rushed in. The smugglers saw that resistance would be vain; but still they resisted; and though, in the agitation of the moment, Ned Ramley's pistol was discharged innocuously, he did not fail to aim it at the head of young William Harris, who was springing towards him. The stout farmer, however, instantly levelled him with the ground by a thundering blow upon the head; and the other two men, after a desperate struggle, were likewise taken and tied.

"Lucky for you it was me, and not my father, Master Ramley," said William Harris. "He'd have blown your brains out; but you're only saved to be hanged, anyhow.—Ay, here he comes!—Stop, stop, old gentleman! he's a prisoner; don't you touch him.—Let the law have the job, as the gentleman said."

"Oh, you accursed villain—oh, you hellish scoundrel," cried old Harris, kept back with difficulty by his son and the rest. "You were one of the foremost of them. But where is the greatest villain of them all?—where's that limb of the devil, young Radford?—I will have him! Let me go, Will—I will have him, I say!"

Ned Ramley laughed aloud: "You wont, though," he answered, bitterly; "he's been gone this half hour, and will be at the sea, and over the sea, before you can catch him.—You may do with me what you like, but he's safe enough."

"Some one ride off and tell the officer what he says!" cried the farmer. But when the intelligence was conveyed to Sir Henry Leyton, he was already aware that some of the men must have made their escape unobserved; for his servant had met Cornet Joyce and the party of dragoons by the way, and with the aid of a number of farm servants from Iden Green and its neighbourhood, the wood had been searched with such strictness, that the pheasants, which were at that time numerous there, had flown out in clouds, as if a battue had been going on. He mistrusted Ned Ramley's information, however; knowing that the hardened villain would find a sort of pride in misleading the pursuers of young Radford, even though taken himself. Riding quickly across to the farm, then, together with Mowle and the Cornet, he interrogated the men separately, but found they were all in the same story, from which they varied not in the least—that Richard Radford had crept out by the hedges near the wood, and had gone first to a place where a horse was in waiting for him, and thence would make straight to the sea-side, where a boat was already prepared. Instant measures to prevent him from executing this plan now became necessary; and Leyton directed the Cornet to hasten away as fast as possible in pursuit, sending information from Woodchurch to every point of the coast where the offender was likely to pass, spreading out his men so as to cover all the roads to the sea, and only leaving at the farm a sufficient guard to secure the prisoners.

On hearing the latter part of this order, however, Farmer Harris exclaimed, "No, no, sir; no need of that. We've taken them, and we'll keep them safe enough. I'll see these fellows into prison myself—ay, and hanged too, please

God! and we'll guard them sure, don't you be afraid."

Leyton looked to Mowle, saying, "I must abide by your decision, Mr. Mowle." But the officer answered: "Oh, you may trust them, sir, quite safely, after all I hear has happened. But I think, Mr. Harris, you had better have just a few men to help you. You've got no place to keep them here; and they must be taken before a magistrate first, before they can be committed."

"Oh, we'll keep them safe enough," replied the farmer. "We'll put them in Goudhurst church, till we can send them off, and, in the meantime, I'll have them up before Squire Broughton. My son's a constable, so they are in proper hands."

"Very well," answered Leyton; "in this case I have no right to interfere; but, of course, you are responsible for their safe custody."

"I say, Mowle," cried Ned Ramley, in his usual daring manner, "bid them give me something to drink, for I'm devilish thirsty; and I'll give you some information, if you will."

Mowle obtained some beer for him, and then demanded, "Well, what is it, Ned?"

"Why, only this," said Ned Ramley, after they had held the beer to his lips, and he had taken a deep draught—"you will have your brains blown out, before ten days are over."

"I am not afraid," replied Mowle, laughing.

"That's right," answered Ned Ramley. "But it will happen; for fifty of us have sworn it. We have had our revenge of your spy, Harding; and we have only you to settle with now."

"Harding!" cried Mowle. "He's no spy of mine.—It was not he that peached, you young scoundrel; it was one of those whom you trusted more than him."

"Ah, well," answered Ned Ramley, indifferently; "then he'll have a sore heart to-night, that he didn't work for. But you'll have your turn yet, Mr. Mowle, so look that you make good use of your brains, for they wont be long in your skull."

"You are a hardened villain," said Sir Henry Leyton. "You had better march them off as fast as you can, my good friends; take them before a magistrate; and above all things, get them to prison ere nightfall, or we may have another rescue."

"No fear, no fear!" answered Farmer Harris. "To rescue a smuggler is one thing—I never liked to see them taken myself—but bloodthirsty villains like these, that would ill use a poor, dear, good girl, and murder her in cold blood,—why, there is not a man in the county would not help to hang them. But I wish, sir, you would go yourself, and see and stop that other great villain. If he isn't hanged too, I don't think I shall ever rest in my bed again."

"I will do my best, depend upon it," replied Leyton; "but I must first, Mr. Harris, go to your house, and see the state of that poor girl. I have known her since she was a child, and feel for her almost as if she were a sister."

"Thank you, sir—thank you!" cried old Harris, shaking him by the hand. "There, boys," he continued, dashing away the tears from his eyes—"make a guard, and take these blackguards off in the middle of you. We'll have them up to Squire Broughton's at once; and then I must go back, too."

On his way to the farm, Leyton desired Mowle to return to Woodchurch, and to wait for him there, taking every step that he might think necessary, with the aid of Captain Irby. "I will not be long," he added.

"Pray don't, sir," rejoined Mowle; "for we have other business to do to-night;" and, sinking his voice to a whisper, he added, "I've got the information I wanted, sir. A part of the goods are certainly at Radford Hall, and if we can seize them there, that, with the deposition of the men at Woodchurch, will bring him in for the whole offence."

"I shall, very likely, overtake you by the way," replied Leyton. "But, at all events, I shall be there before four."

Most such calculations are vain, however. Leyton turned aside to the Harris's farm, where he found poor Kate Clare sinking rapidly. The curate of the parish had been sent for, and, by his advice, Mr. Broughton, the magistrate, who had entered the house but two or three minutes before Leyton himself. Though her voice now scarcely rose above a whisper, she made her dying declaration with clearness and accuracy. It is not necessary here to give any of the details; but, as she concluded, she turned her faint and swimming eyes towards Leyton, saying, "That gentleman, who has always been such a good friend to me and mine, can tell you more, sir, for he came up to my help, just as they shot me."

The magistrate raised his eyes, and inquired, in a low tone, "Who is he?"

"Sir Henry Leyton," replied the poor girl, loud enough for that officer to hear; and thinking that she asked for him, he approached nearer, and stood by Harding's side. Kate raised her hand a little from the bedclothes, as if she would have given it to him; and he took it kindly in his, speaking some words of comfort.

"Thank you, sir—thank you, for all your kindness," said Kate. "I am glad you have come, that I may wish you good-bye, and ask you to be kind to poor Harding, too. It will soon be over now; and you had better all leave me. Not you, Harding—not you.—You must close my eyes, as my poor mother is not here."

A groan burst from the stout seaman's breast; and giving way to all his feelings, he sobbed like a child. According to her desire, Leyton and Mr. Broughton retired from the room; and the young officer informed the magistrate, that the prisoners who had been taken were waiting for examination at his house.

"We shall want your evidence, Sir Henry," said the magistrate. "It is absolutely necessary, if, as I understand, you were eye-witness to the murder."

Leyton saw the propriety of the magistrate's demand, and he yielded immediately. But the investigation was prolonged by several circumstances; and, what between the time that it took up, and that which had been previously spent in the pursuit of the murderers, it was past three o'clock before Leyton mounted his horse at Mr. Broughton's door. He paused for an instant at the gate of the Harris's farm-yard, where a girl was standing with tears in her eyes; but before he could ask any question, she replied to that which was rising to his lips. "She is gone, sir," said the girl—"she is gone. She did not last half-an-hour after you were here."

With a sad heart, Leyton rode on, passing at a quick pace through Harbourne Wood, and not trusting himself to stop at Mrs. Clare's cottage. The windows, however, were closed; and the young officer concluded from that circumstance, that the tidings of her daughter's fate must by this time have reached the childless widow. Not far beyond her gate, he was met by Sir Edward Digby's servant; but eager to arrive at Woodchurch, Leyton did not stop to speak with him, and Somers, turning his horse with the orderly and his old companion, Leyton's servant, gleaned what information he could from them as he went.

Notwithstanding all the speed he could use, however, it was half-past four before Leyton reached Woodchurch; and, on inquiring for Mr. Warde, he found that gentleman had called, but gone away again, saying he would return in an hour.

CHAPTER X.

SUCH as we have described in the last chapter, were the fatal events to which Sir Edward Digby had alluded in the few words he had spoken to Zara Croyland; and it may be needless to explain to the reader, that he had learned the tale from his servant just before he came down to dinner.

Sir Robert Croyland, as we have shown, after some agitation and hesitation, quitted the drawing-room to meet,—the first time for many years—the son of a man, whom, at the instigation of others, he had cruelly persecuted. He paused as soon as he got into the passage, however, to summon courage, and to make up his mind as to the demeanour which he should assume—always a vain and fruitless task; for seldom, if ever, do circumstances allow any man to maintain the aspect which he has predetermined to affect. Sir Robert Croyland resolved to be cold, stately, and repulsive—to treat Sir Henry Leyton as a perfect stranger, and if he alluded to their former intimacy, to cut the conversation short by telling him that, as all the feelings of those days were at an end, he did not wish to revive their memory in any shape. He did not calculate, indeed, upon the peculiar state of Leyton's mind, at the moment—nay, nor even upon the effect of his former favourite's personal appearance upon himself; and when he entered the library and saw the tall, powerful, dignified-looking man, the pale, thoughtful, stern countenance, and the haughty air, he felt all his predeterminations vain.

Leyton, on his part, had done the same as Sir Robert Croyland, and in setting out from Woodchurch had made up his mind to see in the man he went to visit, nothing but Edith's father—to treat him kindly, gently, and with compassion for his weakness, rather than anger at his faults; but as he rode along, and conversed with one who accompanied him thither, the memory of much that Sir Robert Croyland had done in former days, came painfully back upon him, and combining with his treatment of

Edith, raised up bitter and indignant feelings that he could have wished to quell. The scenes which he had passed through that day, too, had given a tone of sternness to his mind which was not usual; and the few minutes he had waited in the library, when every moment seemed of value, added impatience to his other sensations.

The baronet entered as firmly as he could, bowing his head and motioning coldly to a chair. But Leyton did not sit down, gazing for an instant on the countenance of Sir Robert, struck and astonished by the change that he beheld. That steadfast gaze was painful to its object, and sank his spirit still farther; but Leyton, the moment after, began to speak; and the well-known tones of his clear, mellow voice, awakened the recollection of the days when they were once pleasant to hear.

"Sir Robert Croyland," he said, "I have come to you on business of importance, in which it is necessary for you to act immediately in your magisterial capacity."

"I have no clerk with me, sir," answered the baronet, in a hesitating manner; "at this late hour, it is not usual, except under circumstances——"

"The circumstances admit of no delay, Sir

Robert Croyland," replied Leyton. "As the nearest magistrate, I have applied to you in the first instance; and have done so for many other reasons besides your being the nearest magistrate."

"Well, sir, what is your application?" demanded Edith's father. "I wish, indeed, you had applied to somebody else, at this time of night; but I will do my duty—oh, yes, I will do my duty."

"That is all that is requiréd, sir," answered the young officer. "My application is for a warrant to search the house of one Richard Radford; and I have to tender you, on oath, information that customable goods, which have been introduced without the payment of duty, are concealed on his premises.—One moment more, if you please—I have also to apply to you, upon similar evidence, for a warrant to search his house for his son, Richard Radford, charged with murder; and, in the end, if you would allow me to advise you, you would instantly mount your horse, and superintend the search yourself."

There was a marked and peculiar emphasis on the last few words, which Sir Robert Croyland did not understand. The manner was not agreeable to him; but it was scarcely perhaps to be expected that it should be ; for there had been nothing in his own, to invite that kindly candour, which opens heart to heart. All that had of late years passed between him and Sir Henry Leyton, had been of a repulsive kind. For one youthful error, he had not only repelled and shut his house against the son, but he had persecuted, ruined, and destroyed the father, who had no part in that fault. Every reason too, which he had given, every motive he had assigned, for his anger at Henry Leyton's pretensions to Edith's hand, he had set at nought, or forgotten in the case of him whom he had chosen for her husband. Even now, although his manner was wavering and timid, it was cold and harsh ; and it was a hard thing for Henry Leyton to assume the tone of kindness towards Sir Robert Croyland, or to soften his demeanour towards him, with all the busy memories of the past and the feelings of the present thronging upon him, on his first return to the house where he had spent many happy days in youth. I am painting a man, and nothing more ; and he could not, and did not overcome the sensations of human nature.

His words did not please Sir Robert Croyland, but they somewhat alarmed him. Everything that was vague in his present situation, did produce fear; but after a moment's thought, he replied, coldly, "Oh dear no, sir, I do not see that it is at all necessary I should go myself. I really think the application altogether extraordinary, seeing that it comes from, I am led to imagine, the lieutenant-colonel, commanding the —— regiment of dragoons, quartered in this district, who has no primary power, or authority, or even duty in such affairs; but can only act as required by the officers of Customs, to whom he is so far subordinate.—But still I am ready to receive the informations tendered, and then shall decide in regard to my own conduct, as the case may require."

"You are wrong in all respects, but one, Sir Robert Croyland," answered Leyton, at once; "I am empowered to act very differently from any officer who has been in command here before me. If my powers are beyond that which the law authorizes, those who gave them are responsible to their country; but, for an extraordinary case, extraordinary means are requisite; and as I require of you nothing but what the law requires, I shall not pause to argue, whether I am exactly the proper person to make the application. It might easily be made by another, who is without; but I have reasons for what I am doing—and reasons, believe me," he added, after a moment's pause and reflection, "not unfriendly to Sir Robert Croyland."

Again his words and manner were peculiar. Sir Robert Croyland began to feel some apprehension lest he might push his coldness too far. But he did not see how he could change his tone; and he was proceeding, with the same distant reserve, to repeat that he was ready to receive the information in a formal manner, when Leyton suddenly interrupted him, after a severe struggle with himself.

"Sir Robert Croyland," he said, "let us speak as friends. Let griefs and complaints on both sides be forgotten for the moment; let us bury, for the time, seven years in oblivion. Look upon me, if it be but for a few minutes, as the Henry Leyton you knew before anything arose to produce one ill feeling between us; for, believe me, I come to you with kindly sentiments. Your own fate hangs in the balance at this hour. I would decide it favourably for you, if you would let me. But—you must shake off doubt and timidity; you must act boldly and decidedly, and all will be well."

"I do not understand what you mean, sir," cried Sir Robert Croyland, astonished at his change of tone, and without time to collect his ideas, and calculate the probabilities. "My fate!—How can you affect my fate?"

"More than you are aware," answered Leyton; "even now I affect your fate, by giving you the choice of at once proceeding in the line of your duty, against a bad man who has overruled your better nature, too long,—by allowing you to conduct the search, which must be instituted either by yourself or others.—In one word, Sir Robert Croyland, I know all; and would serve you, if you would let me."

"You know all!" exclaimed Edith's father, in a dull, gloomy tone—"you know all! she has told you, then! That explains it—that shows how she retracted her consent—how she was willing to-day to sacrifice her father. You have seen her—you have taught her her part!—Yes, she has betrayed her parent's confidence."

Leyton could bear no more. Himself, he could have heard slandered calmly; but he could not hear such words of her he loved: "It is false!" he said; "she did not betray your confidence! She told me no more than was needful to induce me to release her from bonds she was too faithful and true to break. From her I have heard nothing more—but from others I have heard all; and now, Sir Robert Croyland, you have chosen your part, I have but to call in those who must lay the required information. Our duty must be done, whatever be the consequences; and as you reject the only means of saving yourself from much grief—though, I trust, not the danger you apprehend—we must act without you;" and he rose and walked towards the door.

"Stay, Leyton—stay!" cried Sir Robert Croyland, catching him eagerly by the arm—"yet a moment—yet a moment. You say you know all. Do you know all?—all?—everything?"

"All!—everything!" answered Leyton, firmly; "every word that was spoken—every deed that was done—more than you know yourself."

"Then, at least, you know I am innocent," said the old man.

A calm but grave serenity took the place, on Sir Henry Leyton's countenance, of the impetuous look with which he had last spoken. "Innocent," he said, "of intentional murder; but not innocent of rash and unnecessary anger; and, oh! Sir Robert Croyland—if I must say it—most culpable in the consequences which you have suffered to flow from one hasty act. Mark me; and see the result!—Your own dear child, against your will, is in the hands of a man whom you hate and abhor. You are anxious to make her the wife of a being you condemn and despise! The child of the man that your own hand slew, is now lying a corpse, murdered by him to whom you would give your daughter! Your own life is ——"

"What, Kate!—Kate Clare!" exclaimed Sir Robert Croyland, with a sudden change coming over his countenance—"murdered by Richard Radford!"

"By his own hand, after the most brutal usage," replied Leyton.

Sir Robert Croyland sprang to the bell, and rang it violently, then threw open the door and called aloud—"My horse!—my horse!—saddle my horse!—If it cost me land and living, life and honour, she shall be avenged!" he added, turning to Leyton, and raising his head erect, the first time for many years. "It is over—the folly, and the weakness, and crime, are at an end. I have been bowed and broken; but there is a spark of my former nature yet left. I vowed to God in Heaven, that I would ever protect and be a father to that child, as an atonement—as some—some compensation, however small; and I will keep my vow."

"Oh! Sir Robert," cried Leyton, taking his

hand and pressing it in his, "be ever thus, and how men will love and venerate you!"

The barrier was broken down—the chain which had so long bound him was cast away; and Sir Robert returned Leyton's grasp with equal warmth. "Harry," he said, "I have done you wrong; but I will do so no more. I was driven—I was goaded along the road to all evil, like a beast driven to the slaughter. But you have done wrong, too, young man—yours was the first offence."

"It was," answered Leyton—"I own it—I did do wrong; and I will make no excuse, though youth, and love as true as ever man felt, might afford some. But let me assure you, that I have been willing to make reparation—I have been willing to sacrifice all the brightest hope of years to save you, even now. I assured Edith that I would, when she told me the little she could venture to tell; but it was her misery that withheld me—it was the life-long wretchedness, to which she was doomed if I yielded, that made me resist. Nothing else on earth should have stopped me; but now, Sir Robert, the prospect is more clear for you."

"Nay, do not speak of that," replied Sir Robert Croyland; "I will think of it no more—

I have now chosen my path; and I will pursue it, without looking at the consequences to myself. Let them come when they must come; for once in life, I will do what is just and right."

"And by so doing, my dear sir, you will save yourself," answered Leyton. "Moved by revenge —with no doubt whatsoever of his motive—after a concealment of six years, this base man's accusation will be utterly valueless. Your bare statement of the real circumstances will be enough to dissipate every cloud. I shall require that all his papers be seized; and I have many just reasons for wishing that they should be in your hands."

"I understand you, Harry, and I thank you," said Sir Robert Croyland; "but with my present feelings I would not ——"

"You do not understand me fully, Sir Robert," replied Leyton. "I wish you only to act as you will find just, right, and honourable, and wait for the result. It will be, or I am much mistaken, more favourable to you, personally, than you imagine. Now, as you have decided on the true and upright course, let us lose no time in carrying it into execution. I will call in the men who have to lay the information; and when you have received it, I will place before you depositions which will justify the most vigorous measures against both father and son. In regard to the latter, I must act under your authority in my military capacity, as I have no civil power there; but in regard to the former, I am already called upon, by the officers of the revenue, to aid them in entering his house by force, and searching it thoroughly."

"Call them in, Harry—call them in!" replied Sir Robert Croyland; "every man is justified by the law in apprehending a murderer. But you shall have full authority.—Kate Clare!—How could this have happened?"

"I will explain, as we ride on," answered Leyton, going to the door; and speaking to one of the servants who was standing in the hall, he added, "Desire Mr. Mowle to walk in, and bring the boy with him."

In another minute, Mowle entered the room with another man, holding by the arm the boy Ray, whom the smugglers had chosen to denominate Little Starlight. He came, apparently, unwillingly; for though ever ready, for money, to spy and to inform secretly, he had a great abhorrence of being brought publicly forward; and when on coming to Mowle that evening with more information—he was detained and told he must go before a magistrate, he had made every possible effort to escape.

He was now somewhat surprised, on being brought forward after Mowle had laid the information, to find that he was not questioned upon any point affecting the smuggling transactions which had lately taken place, as the evidence upon that subject was sufficient without his testimony. But in regard to the proceedings of young Radford, and to the place where he was concealed, he was interrogated closely. It was all in vain, however. To obtain a straightforward answer from him was impossible; and although Mowle repeated distinctly that the boy had casually said, the murderer of poor Kate Clare had gone to his father's house, Little Starlight lied and prevaricated at every word, and impudently, though not unskilfully attempted to put another meaning on his previous admission.

As time was wearing away, however, Sir Henry Leyton, at length, interposed—"I think it is unnecessary, Sir Robert," he said, "to push this inquiry further at present. As the whole house and premises must be searched on other grounds, we shall discover the villain if he is there. Mr. Mowle and I have adopted infallible means, I think, to prevent his escaping from any point of the coast; and the magistrates at every port were this evening furnished with such information that, if they act with even a moderate degree of ability, he must be taken."

"Besides, sir," rejoined Mowle, "the frigate has come round; and she will take care that, with this wind, not a boat big enough to carry him over shall get out. We had better set out, your worship, if you please; for if old Radford gets an inkling of what is going on, he will double upon us some way."

"I am quite ready," said Sir Robert Croyland. "I will call my clerk to accompany us as we go, in case of any further proceedings being necessary. We must pass through the village where he lives."

With a firm step he moved towards the door; and, strange as it may seem, though for six years, while supposing he was taking the only means of self-preservation, he had lived in constant terror and anxiety, he felt no fear, no trepidation now, when he had determined to do what was right at every personal risk. An enfeebling spell seemed to have been taken off his mind; and the lassitude of doubt and indecision was gone. But such is almost always the result, even upon the nerves of our corporeal frame, of a strong effort of mental energy. It is one thing certainly to resolve, and another to do; but the very act of resolution, if it be sincerely exerted, affords a degree of vigour, which is sure to produce as great results as the means at our disposal can accomplish. Energetic determination will carry men through things that seem impossible, as a bold heart will carry them over Alps, that, viewed from their base, appear insurmountable.

Sir Robert Croyland did not venture into the drawing-room before he went; but he told the butler, who was waiting in the hall, to inform Sir Edward Digby and the family that he had been called away on business, and feared he should not return till a late hour; and having left this message, he went out upon the terrace. He found there a number of persons assembled, with some twenty or thirty of the dragoons. Five or six officers of the Customs were present, besides Mowle; but the darkness was too great to admit of their faces being seen; and Sir Robert Croyland mounted without speaking to any one. Sir Henry Leyton paused for an instant to give orders, that the boy should be taken back to Woodchurch, and kept there under a safe guard. He then spoke a few words to Digby's servant, Somers, and springing on his horse placed himself at Sir Robert Croyland's side.

The night was as dark as either of the two which had preceded it; the same film of cloud covered the sky; not a star was to be seen; the moon was far below the horizon; and slowly the whole party moved on, two and two abreast, through the narrow lanes and tortuous roads of that part of the country. It halted for a minute in the nearest village, while Sir Robert Croyland stopped at his clerk's house, and directed him to follow as fast as possible to Mr. Radford's; and then, resuming their march, the dragoons, and those who accompanied them, wound on for between four or five miles further, when, as they turned the angle of a wood, some lights, apparently proceeding from the windows of a house half way up a gentle slope, were seen shining out in the midst of the darkness.

"Halt!" said Sir Henry Leyton; and before he proceeded to give his orders, for effectually surrounding the house and grounds of Mr. Radford, he gazed steadfastly for a moment or two upon the building which contained her who was most dear to him, and whose heart he well knew was at that moment wrung with the contention of many a painful feeling. "I promised her I would bring her aid, dear girl," he thought, "and so I have.—Thanks be to God, who has enabled me!"

Sir Robert Croyland, too, gazed—with very different feelings, it is true, but still with a stern determination that was not shaken in the least. It seemed, when he thought of Kate Clare, that he was atoning to the spirit of the father, by seeking to avenge the child; and the whole tale of her wrongs and death, which he had heard from Leyton, as they came, had raised the desire of so doing almost to an enthusiasm. Human passions and infirmities, indeed, will mingle with our best feelings; and as he gazed upon Mr. Radford's house, and remembered all that he had endured for the last six years, he said to himself, with some bitterness, "That man shall now taste a portion of the same cup he has forced upon others."

Sir Henry Leyton woke from his reverie sooner than his companion; and turning his horse, he spoke for a few moments with Mowle, somewhat longer with another person wrapped in a dark horseman's coat behind, and then gave various distinct orders to the dragoons, who immediately separated into small parties, and, taking different roads, placed themselves in such positions as to command every approach to the house. Then riding forward with Sir Robert Croyland, the officers of Customs, and one or two soldiers, he turned up the little avenue which led from the road, consulting with Edith's father as he went. At about a couple of hundred yards from the house he paused, turning his head and saying to Mowle, "You had better, I think, all dismount; and, making fast the horses, get behind the nearest laurels and evergreens, while Sir Robert and I ride on alone, and ask admission quietly. When the door is opened, you can come up and make yourselves masters of the servants till the search is over. I do not anticipate any resistance; but if the young man be really here, it may be made."

He then rode on with the baronet at a quicker pace, the noise of their horses' feet, as they trotted on and approached the great doors, covering the sound of the movements of the party they left behind.

The house, to which the actual possessor had given the name of Radford Hall, was an old-fashioned country mansion, and presented, like many another building at that time, several large, iron hooks, standing out from the brick-work on each side of the door-way, on which it was customary for visitors on horseback to hang their rein while they rang the bell, or till a servant could be called to take them to the stable. Sir Robert Croyland was acquainted with this peculiarity of the house, though Leyton was not, and he whispered to his companion—"Let us hook up our horses, before we ring."

This was accordingly done; and then taking the long iron handle of the bell, Leyton pulled it gently. A minute or two after, a step sounded in the hall, and a servant appeared—a stout, red-faced, shrewd-looking fellow, who at first held the great door only half open. As soon, however, as he saw Sir Robert Croyland's face, he threw it back, replying, in answer to the baronet's question as to whether Mr. Radford was at home, "Yes, Sir Robert, he has been home this hour."

Leyton had stood back, and, in the darkness, the man did not see him, or took him for a groom; but when the young officer advanced, and the uniform of the dragoon regiment became apparent, Mr. Radford's servant suddenly stretched his hand towards the door again, as if about to throw it violently to. But Leyton's strong grasp was on his shoulder in a moment. "You are my prisoner," he said, in a low tone; "not a word—not a syllable, if you would not suffer for it. No harm will happen to you, if you are only quiet."

At the same moment, Mowle and the rest came running across the lawn, and, giving the man into their hands, Leyton entered the house with Sir Robert Croyland.

CHAPTER XI.

About an hour before the event took place, which we have last related, Edith Croyland sat in a small drawing-room at the back of Mr Radford's house, in which she had been kept captive—for we may well use that term—ever since her removal from Mr. Croyland's. Her first day had been spent in tears and indignation; for immediately after her arrival, on finding that her father was not really there, she became convinced that she had been deceived, and naturally doubted that it was with his consent she had been removed. Nor had Mr. Radford's manner at all tended to do away with this impression. He laughed at her remonstrances and indignation, treated her tears with cold indifference, and told his servants, before her face, that she was on no account to be suffered to go out, or to see any one but Sir Robert Croyland. In other respects, he treated her well—did all in his power to provide for her comfort; and, as his whole establishment was arranged upon a scale of luxury and extravagance rarely met with in the old country houses of the gentry of that time, none of the materials of that which is commonly called comfort were wanting.

But it was the comfort of the heart which Edith required, and did not find. Mr. Radford handed her down to dinner himself, and with as much ceremonious politeness as he could show, seated her at the end of his ostentatious table: but Edith did not eat. She retired at night to the downy bed prepared for her: but Edith did not sleep. Thus passed the first day and the morning of the second; and when, about noon, Sir Robert Croyland arrived, he found her pale and wan with anxiety and watching; and he left her paler still; for he resisted all her entreaties to take her thence; and her last hope of relief was gone.

He had spoken kindly—tenderly, indeed; he had even shed tears; but his mind at the time of his visit was still in a state of suspense, irritated by injuries and insult, but not yet roused by indignation to dare the worst that Mr. Radford could do; and, though he heard her express her determination never to marry Richard Radford unless set free from her vows to Henry Leyton, without remonstrance, only begging her to keep that resolution secret till the last moment, yet, with the usual resource of weakness, he sought to postpone the evil hour by seeming to enter into all his enemy's views.

Thus had passed Edith's time; and it is unnecessary to enter into a more detailed account of her thoughts and feelings previous to the period we have mentioned—namely, one hour before the arrival of her father and Henry Leyton at the door of the house. She was sitting, then, in that small back drawing room, with her fair cheek leaning on her hand, her eyes bent down upon the table, and her mind busy with the present and the future. "It is foolish," she thought, "thus to alarm myself. No harm can happen. They dare not show me any violence; and no clergyman in England will venture to proceed with the service against my loud dissent. My uncle, and Leyton too, must soon hear of this, and will interfere.—I will not give way to such terrors any more."

As she thus meditated, she heard a rapid step

upon the great stairs; and the next moment Mr. Radford entered—booted, spurred, and dusty, as from a journey, and with a heavy horsewhip in his hand. His face betrayed more agitation than she had ever seen it display. There was a deep line between his brows, as if they had been long bent into such a frown, that they could not readily be smoothed again. His long upper-lip was quivering with a sort of impatient vehemence that would not be restrained; and his eye was flashing, as if under the influence of some strong passion.

"Well, Miss Croyland," he said, throwing his horsewhip down upon the table, and casting himself into a chair, "I hope they have made you comfortable during my absence?"

Edith merely bowed her head, without reply.

"Well, that's civil!" cried Mr. Radford; "but I think every body is going mad, and so it is no wonder that women do! Miss Croyland, I have a piece of news for you—there's going to be a wedding in our house, to-night!"

Still Edith was silent, and looked towards the fire.

"I tell you of the fact," continued Mr. Radford, "because it may be necessary for you to make some little preparation for your journey.

I don't know whether you hear or not; but you are to be married to my son, to-night. It is now nine; the clergyman and Richard will be here by eleven; and the marriage will take place half an hour before twelve. So you have two hours and a half to prepare."

"You are mistaken altogether, Mr. Radford," replied Edith, in as firm a tone as she could assume. "It is not my intention to marry your son at all. I have often told you so—I now repeat it."

"You do, do you!" exclaimed Mr. Radford, giving her a furious glance across the table; "then I will tell you something, young woman. Your consent was given to your father; and I will have no trifling backwards and forwards. Circumstances have arisen to-day—curses be upon them all!—which render it necessary that the marriage should take place four-and-twenty hours before it was first fixed, and it shall take place, by ——!" and he added a terrible oath.

"You will find it will not take place, Mr. Radford," replied Edith, in the same tone as before, "for, in the first place, I never did consent. My father left me fainting, without waiting to hear what I had to say, or he would not have so deceived himself."

"Then he shall die the death of a felon," cried Mr. Radford, "and you yourself shall be the person to put the rope round his neck."

"Whatever be the consequences, I shall be firm," replied Edith; "but at the same time, let me tell you, I do not believe you have the power you suppose. You may bring a false accusation —an accusation you know to be false; but such things are never so well prepared but they are discovered at last; and so it will be in your case."

"A false accusation!" exclaimed Mr. Radford vehemently—"an accusation I know to be false! I'll soon show you that, girl;" and starting up from his seat, he hurried out of the room.

Contrary to Edith's expectation, Mr. Radford was absent for a long time; but when he returned he had several papers in his hand, some apparently freshly written, and one which bore the yellow marks of age. His face was stern and resolute, but displayed less excitement than when he left her. He entered with a slow step, leaving the door partly open behind him, seated himself, and gazed at her for a moment, then spread out the small yellow paper on the table, but held his hand tight upon the lower part, as if he feared she might snatch it up and destroy it.

"There, look at that, Miss Croyland!" he said; "you spoke of false accusations; look at that, and be ashamed of bringing them yourself."

Edith gave a glance towards it with a sensation of awe, but did not attempt to read it. Her eye rested upon the words, "Deposition of—" and upon a stain of blood at the bottom of the page, and she turned away with a shudder. "I have heard of it before," she answered, "yet every word in it may be false."

"False, or not false," replied Mr. Radford, "it sends your father to gaol to-morrow, and to the gallows a month after—if you do not instantly sign that!" and he laid another freshly written page open before her.

Edith took it in her hand, and read—"I hereby consent and promise, when called upon, to marry Richard Radford, junior, Esquire, the son of Richard Radford, of Radford Hall."

"You have your choice, Miss Croyland," continued her persecutor, in a low and bitter tone, "either to save your father, or to put him to death with your own hands; for I swear, by all that I hold sacred, that if you do not instantly sign that paper—ay, and fulfil its engagement, I will send off this deposition to the bench of magistrates, with the letter I have just written, giving an account of all the circumstances, and explaining how, out of weak kindness and friendship for Sir Robert Croyland, I have been prevailed upon to keep back the information until now. Do not deceive yourself, and think that his fortune or his station will save him. A peer of the realm has been hanged before now for the murder of his own servant. Neither must you suppose that upon that deposition alone rests the proof of his guilt. There was other evidence given at the Coroner's inquest, all bearing upon the same point, which requires but this light, to be made plain. The threats your father previously used, the falsehoods he told regarding where he had been—all these things can be proved, for I have taken care to preserve that evidence."

"That was like a friend, indeed!" murmured Edith; "but such are the friendships of the world."

"I am acting like a friend to you, Miss Croyland," rejoined Mr. Radford, apparently neither touched nor hurt by her words, "in letting you see clearly your father's situation, while I give you the opportunity of saving him if you will. Do as you please—there is the paper. Sign it if you like; but sign it quickly; for this night brings all tergiversation to an end. I will have no more of it; and five minutes decides your father's life or death. Do not say I do it. It is you. His pardon is before you. You have nothing to do but to put your name. If you do not, you sign his death warrant!"

"Five minutes!" said Edith, with her heart beating violently.

"Ay, five minutes," answered Mr. Radford, who saw, from the wild look of her beautiful eyes, and the ashy paleness of her cheek and lips, how powerfully he had worked upon her—"five minutes, no longer;" and he laid his watch upon the table. Then, turning somewhat ostentatiously to a small fixed writing-desk, which stood near, he took up a stick of sealing-wax, and laid it down beside the letter he had written, as if determined not to lose a moment beyond the period he had named.

Edith gazed upon the paper for an instant, agitated and trembling through her whole frame; but her eye fell upon the name of Richard Radford. His image rose up before her, recalling all the horror that she felt whenever he was in her presence; then came the thought of Leyton, and of her vows to him yet uncancelled. "Richard Radford!" she said to herself—"Richard Radford!—marry him—vow that I will love him—call God to witness, when I know I shall abhor him more and more—when I love another? I cannot do it—I will not do it!" and she pushed the paper from her, saying, aloud, "No, I will not sign it!"

"Very well," said Mr. Radford—"very well. Your parent's blood be upon your head;" and he proceeded to fold up slowly the deposition he had shown her, in the letter he had written. But he stopped in the midst; and then, abandoning the calm, low tone, and stern but quiet demeanour which he had lately used, he started up, striking the table violently with his hand, and exclaiming, in a loud and angry tone, "Wretched, miserable girl, dare you bring upon your head the guilt of parricide? What was the curse of Cain to that? How will you bear the day of your father's trial—ay, how bear the day of his death—the lingering agony of his imprisonment—the public shame of the court of justice—the agony of the gallows and the cord?—the proud Sir Robert Croyland become the gaze of hooting boys, the spectacle of the rude multitude, expiring, through his daughter's fault, by the hand of the common hangman!

Ay, think of it all, for in another minute it will be too late! Once gone from my hand, this paper can never be recalled."

Edith uttered a faint cry; but at the same moment a voice behind Mr. Radford said, "Nor can it, now!" and Sir Robert Croyland himself laid his hand upon the papers.

Mr. Radford turned round fiercely, and was darting forward to seize them from him; but he was held back by a more powerful arm; and the baronet went on, in a voice grave and sad, but firm and strong—"Sir Henry Leyton," he said, "I give these papers into your hands to do with exactly as you may think right, as a man of honour, a gentleman, and a respecter of the law. I ask not to hold them for one moment."

"Do not struggle, sir,—do not struggle!" cried Leyton, holding Mr. Radford fast by the collar—"you are a prisoner."

"A prisoner!" exclaimed Mr. Radford. "What! in my own house—a magistrate!"

"Anywhere, sir," answered Leyton; "and for the time, you are a magistrate no longer.—Ho! without there!—send some one in!"

Edith had sunk down in her seat; for she knew not whether to rejoice or grieve. The first feeling undoubtedly was joy; but the next was bitter apprehension for her father. At first she covered her eyes with her hands; for she thought to hear the terrible truth proclaimed aloud; but when she looked up, Sir Robert Croyland's face was so calm, so resolute, so unlike what it had ever appeared of late years, that fear gave way to surprise, and surprise began to verge into hope. As that bright flame arose again in her heart, she started up, and cast herself upon her father's bosom, murmuring, while the tears flowed rapidly from her eyes, "Are you safe—are you safe?"

"I know not, my dear child," replied Sir Robert Croyland; "but I am now doing my duty, and that gives me strength."

In the meantime, a dragoon had appeared at the door, and as soon as Mr. Radford beheld him, he exclaimed, "This is a base and infamous plot to defeat the ends of justice. I understand it all: the military power called in, right willingly, I have no doubt, to take away the documents which prove that felon's guilt. But this shall be bitterly repaid, and I hold you responsible, sir, for the production of these papers."

"Certainly, Mr. Radford," replied Leyton, with a calm smile, "I will be responsible. But as you object to the military power, we will hand you over to the civil. Hart," he continued, speaking to the soldier, "call up Mowle or Birchett, or any of the other officers, and let them bring one of the constables with them, for this is not purely a case for the Customs. Then tell Serjeant Shaw to bring on his men from the back, as I directed, seeing that nothing—not an inch of ground, not a shed, not a tool-house, remains unexamined."

"Of what am I accused, sir, that you dare to pursue such a course in my house?" demanded Mr. Radford.

"Of murder, sir," replied Sir Henry Leyton.

"Murder!" exclaimed Mr. Radford, and then burst into an affected laugh.

"Yes, sir," replied the young officer; "and you may find it not so much a jest as you suppose; for though the law, in consequence of the practices of yourself and others, has slept long ineffective, it is not dead. I say for murder! as an accessory before the fact, to the armed resistance of lawful authority, in which his majesty's subjects have been killed in the execution of their duty; and as an accessory after the fact, in harbouring and comforting the actual culprits, knowing them to be such."

Mr. Radford's countenance fell; for he perceived that the matter was much more serious than he at first supposed. He trusted, indeed, from the laxity with which the law had lately been carried into execution, that he might escape from the gravest part of the charge; but still, if Sir Henry Leyton was in a condition to prove the participation of which he accused him, in the crimes that had been committed, nothing short of transportation for life could be anticipated. But he had other sources of anxiety. His wretched son, he expected to present himself every minute; and well aware of the foul deed which Richard Radford had that morning perpetrated, and of his person having been recognised, he was perfectly certain, that his apprehension would take place. He would have given worlds to speak for a single instant with one of his own servants; but none of them appeared; and while these thoughts were passing rapidly through his brain, the officer Birchett entered the room with a constable, and several other persons followed them in. He was startled from his reverie, however, by Sir Henry Leyton's voice demanding—"Have you brought handcuffs, constable?"

"Oh, ay, sir," answered the man, "I've got the bracelets."

"Good evening, Mr. Radford," said Birchett; "we have hold of you at last, I fancy."

Mr. Radford was silent, and the young officer demanded, "Have you found anything else, Birchett?"

"Oh yes, sir, plenty," answered Birchett, "and besides the run goods, things enough to prove all the rest even if we had not proof sufficient before—one of your own dragoon's swords, sir, that must have been snatched up from some poor fellow who was killed. Corporal Hart says, he thinks it belonged to a man named Green."

"Well, there is your prisoner," replied Leyton, —"you and the constable must take care that he be properly secured. No unnecessary harshness, I beg; but you know how rescue is sometimes attempted, and escape effected. You had better remove him to another room; for we must have all the papers and different articles of smuggled goods brought hither."

"I protest against the whole of this proceeding," exclaimed Mr. Radford, on whom the constable was now unceremoniously fixing a pair of handcuffs, "and I beg every body will take notice of my protest. This person, who is, I suppose, a military officer, is quite going beyond his duty, and acting as if he were a civil magistrate."

"I am acting under the orders and authority of a magistrate, sir," replied Sir Henry Leyton, "and according to my instructions.—Dear Edith," he continued, crossing over to her, and taking her hand as she still clung to her father; for all that I have described had taken place with great rapidity—"you had better go into another room till this is over. We shall have some papers to examine, and I trust another prisoner before the search is finished.—Had she not better retire, Sir Robert?"

But Mr. Radford raised his voice again, as the constable was moving him towards the door, exclaiming, "At all events, I claim my right to witness all these extraordinary proceedings. It is most unjust and illegal for you to seize and do what you will with my private papers, in my absence."

"It is a very common occurrence," said Sir Henry Leyton, "in criminal cases like your own."

"Let him remain—let him remain!" said Sir Robert Croyland. "He can but interrupt us a little.—Oh, here is the clerk at last!—Now, Edith, my love, you had better go; these are no scenes for you."

Leyton took her by the hand, and led her

to the door, bending down his head and whispering as he went, "Be under no alarm, dear girl. All will go well."

"Are you sure, Harry—are you sure?" asked Edith, gazing anxiously in his face.

"Certain," he replied; "your father's decision has saved him."

As he spoke, there was a violent ringing at the bell; and Mr. Radford said to himself, "It is that unhappy boy; he will be taken, to a certainty." But the next instant, he thought, "No—no, he would never come to the front door. It must be some more of their party."

Sir Robert Croyland, in the meantime, seated himself at the end of the table, and handed over a number of papers, which Leyton had given him at his own house, to the clerk, who, by his direction, seated himself near. "I have no objection, Mr. Radford," he said, turning to the prisoner, "that you should hear read, if you desire it, the depositions on which I have granted a warrant for your apprehension, and, at the requisition of the officers of Customs, have authorized your premises to be searched for the smuggled goods, a part of which has been found upon them. The depositions are those of a man named George Jones, since dead, and of Michael

Scalesby, and Edward Larchant, at present in the hands of justice; and the information is laid by John Mowle and Stephen Birchett."

At the recital of the names of several of the men whom he himself had furnished with arms and directions, Mr. Radford's heart sunk; but the moment after, a gleam of bitter satisfaction sprang up in his breast, as the door opened, and Mr. Zachary Croyland entered, exclaiming, "How's this—how's this? I came to take a dove out of a hawk's nest, and here I find the dogs unearthing a fox."

"I am very glad you are come, sir," replied Mr. Radford, before any one else could speak; "for, though you are the brother of that person sitting there, you are a man of honour, and an honest man——"

"More than I can say for you, Radford," grumbled Mr. Croyland.

"And, moreover, a magistrate for this county," continued Mr. Radford.

"I never act—I never act!" cried the old gentleman. "I never have acted; I never will act."

"But in this case I shall insist upon your acting," said the prisoner; "for your brother, who is now proceeding thus virulently against me, does it to shield himself from a charge of murder, which he knew I was about to bring against him."

"Fiddlesticks' ends!" cried Mr. Croyland. "This is what people call turning the tables, I think. But it wont succeed with me, my good friend. I am an old bird—a very old bird, indeed—and I don't like chaff at all, Radford. If you have any charge to make against my brother, you must make it where you are going. I'll have nothing to do with it. I always knew him to be a fool; but never suspected him of being anything else."

"At all events," said Mr. Radford, in a gloomy tone, "since simple justice is denied me at all hands, I require that the papers which have been seized in this house, be placed in proper hands, and duly authenticated. The important evidence of the crime of which I charge him, has been given by your brother, sir, to one who has but too great an interest, I believe, to conceal or destroy it. I say it boldly, those papers are not safe in the keeping of Sir Henry Leyton; and I demand that they be given up, duly marked by the clerk, and signed by myself, and some independent person."

Leyton's eyes flashed for a moment, at the insinuation which the prisoner threw out; but he overcame his anger instantly, and took the papers which had been handed him, from his pocket, saying, "I will most willingly resign these documents, whatever they may be. Mr. Croyland, this person seems to wish that you should keep them, rather than myself; but here is another paper on the table, which may throw some light upon the whole transaction;" and he took up the written promise, which Mr. Radford had been urging Edith to sign—and on which his own eyes had been fixed during the last few minutes—and handed it, with the rest, to her uncle.

"Stay, stay a moment!" said Mr. Croyland, putting on his spectacles. "I will be responsible for the safe keeping of nothing of which I do not know the contents;" and he proceeded to read aloud the engagement to wed Richard Radford, which Edith had rejected. "Ay, a precious rascally document, indeed!" said the old gentleman, when he had concluded; "written in the hand of the said Richard Radford, Esq., senior, and which, I suppose, Miss Croyland refused to sign under any threats. Be so good as to put your name on that, at the back, Mr. Clerk. I will mark it, too, that there be no mistake."

"And now, sir, since you have read the one, will you be good enough to read the other?" exclaimed Mr. Radford, with a triumphant smile. "Even-handed justice, if you please, Mr. Zachary Croyland; the enclosure first, then the letter, if you will. I see there are a multitude of persons present; I beg they will all attend."

"I will read it certainly," replied Mr. Croyland, drawing one of the candles somewhat nearer. "It seems to be somewhat indistinct."

Sir Robert Croyland leaned his head upon his hand, and covered his eyes; and several persons pressed forward, to hear what seemed of importance—in the eyes of the prisoner, at least.

Mr. Croyland ran over the writing, as a preliminary to reading it aloud; but, as he did so, his countenance fell, and he paused and hesitated. The next moment, however, he exclaimed, "No, hang it! It shall be read—'The deposition of William Clare, now lying at the point of death, and with the full assurance that he has not many minutes to live, made before Richard Radford, Esquire, J. P.; this 24th day of September, in the year of grace 17—;" and he proceeded to read, with a voice occasionally wavering indeed, but in general firm and clear, the formal setting forth of the same tale which the reader has heard before, in the statement of Sir Robert Croyland to his daughter.

His brother paused, and held the paper in his hand for a moment after he had done, while Leyton, who had been standing close beside him, bore a strange, almost sarcastic smile upon his lip, which strongly contrasted with the sad and solemn expression of Mr. Croyland's countenance.

"What is this great red blot just below the man's name?" asked the old gentleman, at length, looking to Mr. Radford.

"That, sir," replied the prisoner, in a calm, grave tone, which had much effect upon the hearers, "is the poor fellow's own blood, as I held him up to sign the declaration. He had been pressing his right hand upon the wound, and where it rested on the paper it gave that bloody witness to the authenticity of the document."

There was something too fine in the reply, and Mr. Croyland repeated, "Bloody witness!—authenticity of the document!"

But Leyton stretched out his hand, saying, "Will you allow me to look at the paper, Mr. Croyland?" and then added, as soon as he received it, "Can any one tell me whether William Clare was left-handed?"

"No!" replied Sir Robert Croyland, suddenly raising his head—"no, he was not.—Why do you ask?"

"That I can answer for," said the constable, coming forward, "for he carved the stock of a gun for me; and I know he never used his left hand when he could use his right one."

"Why do you ask, Harry?—why do you ask?" exclaimed Mr. Croyland.

"Because, my dear sir," answered Leyton, aloud and clear, "this is the print of the thumb of a man's right hand. To have made it at all, he must have held the paper with his right, while he signed with his left, and even then, he could have done it with difficulty, as it is so near the signature, that his fingers would not have room to move;" and as he ended, he fixed his eyes sternly on Mr. Radford's face.

The prisoner's countenance had changed

several times while Sir Henry Leyton spoke, first becoming fiery red, then deadly pale, then red again.

"However it happened, so it was," he said, doggedly.

"Well!" exclaimed Mr. Croyland, sharply, "your evidence will fetch what it is worth!—I hope, clerk, you have got down Mr. Radford's statement."

"He has written the same down here, your worship," replied the man, pointing to the letter in which the deposition had been enclosed, and which, having been cast down by Mr. Zachary, had been busily read by the clerk.

"Well, then, we will read that too," observed the old gentleman. "Silence there!" he continued; for there was a good deal of noise at the side of the room, as the different persons present conversed over the events that were passing; "but first, we had better docket this commodity which we have just perused. Mr. Clerk, will you have the goodness to sign it also—on the back?"

"Stay," said a voice from behind the rest, "let me sign it first;" and the man who had accompanied Leyton thither, wrapped in the dark horseman's coat, advanced between Mr. Croyland and the clerk.

" Any one that likes—any one that likes," answered the former. " Ah, is that you, my old friend ?"

Both Mr. Radford and Sir Robert Croyland gazed, with looks of surprise not unmingled with more painful feelings, on the countenance of Mr. Warde, though each doubted his identity with one whom they had known in former years. But, without noticing any one, the strange-looking old man took the paper from the clerk, dipped the pen in the ink, and, in a bold, free hand, wrote some words upon the back.

" Ha, what is this?" cried Mr. Croyland, taking the paper, and reading—" An infamous forgery—Henry Osborn !"

" Villain, you are detected !" cried the person who has been called Mr. Warde. " I wrote from a distant land to warn you, that I was present when you knelt by William Clare—that I heard all—that I marked you try to prompt the dying man to an accusation he would not make—that I saw you stain the paper with his blood—ay, and sign it, too, after life had quitted him—I wrote to warn you; for I suspected you, from all I heard of your poor tool's changed conduct; and I gave you due notice, that if you ceased not, the day of retribution would arrive.

It is come; and I am here, though you thought me dead! All your shifts and evasions are at an end. There is no collusion here—there is no personal interest. I have not conversed with that weak man for many years—and he it was who persecuted my sister's husband unto death!"

"At his suggestion—from his threats!" exclaimed Sir Robert Croyland, pointing with his hand to Mr. Radford.

"Take me away," said the prisoner, turning to the constable—"I am faint—I am sick—take me away!"

Mr. Croyland nodded his head; and, supported by the constable and Birchett, Mr. Radford was led into the adjoining room.

The scene that followed is indescribable. It was all confusion; every one spoke at once; some strove to make themselves heard above the rest; some seemed little to care whether they were heard or not; if any man thought he could fix another's attention, he tried to converse with him apart—many fixed upon the person nearest; but one or two endeavoured to make others hear across the room; and all order and common form were at an end.

I have said every one spoke; but I should

have made one exception. Sir Robert Croyland talked eagerly with his brother, and said a few low words to Mr. Osborn; but Leyton remained profoundly silent for several minutes. The din of many voices did not seem to disturb him; the strange turn that events had taken, appeared to produce no surprise; but he remained fixed to the same spot, with his eyes bent upon the table, and his mind evidently absent from all that was passing round. It was the abstraction of profound emotion; the power which the heart sometimes exercises over the mind, in withdrawing all its perceptions and its operative faculties from external things, to fix them concentrated upon some great problem within. At length, however, a sense of higher duties made him shake off the thoughts of his own fate and situation—of the bright and glorious hopes that were rising out of the previous darkness, like the splendour of the coming star after a long night—of the dreams of love and joy at length—of the growing light of "trust in the future," still faintly overshadowed by the dark ojects of the past. With a quick start, as if he had awakened from sleep, he looked round, and demanded of one of the soldiers, many of whom were in the room, "Have you found the person accused—Richard

Radford, I mean—has any one been taken in the premises and the house, besides the servants ?"

"Yes, sir, a person just arrived in a post-chaise," replied the sergeant.

"We must have order, Sir Robert," continued Leyton, his powerful voice rising above the din; "there is much more to be done! Clear the room of your men, sergeant. They are not wanted here—but stay, I will speak with Mr. Haveland;" and he went out, followed by the sergeant and some half-dozen of the dragoons, who had accompanied their non-commissioned officer into the room.

Leyton soon returned; but the precautions he had gone to enforce were vain. The person who had arrived in the chaise, proved to be a somewhat disreputable clergyman from a distant parish. Young Richard Radford was not taken; another fate awaited him. A man, indeed, on horseback, was seen to approach the grounds of Radford Hall towards eleven o'clock; but the lights, that were apparent through many windows, seemed to startle him, as he rode along the road. He paused for a moment, and gazed, and then advanced more slowly; but the eagerness of the small guard at that point, perhaps, frustrated their object, for it is not certain to this day who the person was. When he again halted, and seemed to hesitate, they dashed out after him; but instantly setting spurs to his horse, he galloped off into the woods; and knowing the country better than they did, he was soon lost to their pursuit.

In the meantime, the result of the search in Mr. Radford's house was made known, in a formal manner, to the party assembled in the small drawing room. Abundant evidence was found of his having been implicated in all the most criminal parts of the late smuggling transactions; and the business of the night concluded, by an order to remand him, to be brought before the bench of magistrates on the following day; for Sir Robert Croyland declined to commit him on his own responsibility.

"He has preferred a charge against me," he said, in the same firm tone he had lately assumed—"let us see whether he will sustain it to-morrow."

Before all was concluded, it was near midnight; and then every one rose to depart. Mr. Croyland eagerly asked for Edith, saying he would convey her home in his carriage; but Leyton interposed, replying, "We will bring her to you in a moment, my dear friend.—Sir Robert, it may be as well that you and I should seek Miss Croyland alone. I think I saw her maid below."

"Certainly," answered her father, "let us go, my dear Henry, for it is growing very late."

Mr. Croyland smiled, saying, "Well, well, so be it;" and the other two left the room. They found Edith, after some search, seated in the dining hall. She looked pale and anxious; but the expression of Leyton's face relieved her of her worst apprehensions—not that it was joyful; for there was a touch of sadness in it; but she knew that his aspect could not be such, if her father's life were in any real danger.

Leyton advanced towards her at once, even before her father, took her hand in his, and kissed it tenderly. "I told you, dearest Edith," he said, "that I would bring you aid; and I have, thank God, been able to redeem that promise; but now I have another task to perform. Your father's safety is placed beyond doubt—his innocence made clear; and your happiness, beloved one, is not sacrificed. The chance of endangering that happiness was the only cause of my not doing what, perhaps, you desired for his sake—what I do now. Sir Robert Croyland, I did wrong in years long past—in boyhood and the intemperance of youthful love and hope—by engaging your daughter to myself by vows, which she has nobly though painfully kept. As an atonement to you, as a satisfaction to my own sense of right, I now, as far as in me lies, set her free from those engagements, leaving to her own self how she will act, and to you how you will decide. Edith, beloved, you are free, as far as I can make you so; and, Sir Robert, I ask your forgiveness for the wrong act I once committed."

Edith Croyland turned somewhat pale, and looked at her father earnestly; but Sir Robert did not answer for a moment.—Was it that he hesitated?—No; but there was an oppressive weight at his heart, when he thought of all that he had done—all that he had inflicted, not only on the man before him, but on others guiltless of all offence, which seemed almost to stop its beating. But at length, he took Edith's hand and put it in Leyton's, saying, in a low, tremulous voice, "She is yours, Henry—she is yours; and, oh, forgive the father for the daughter's sake!"

CHAPTER XII.

THERE was a solitary light in an upstairs window of Farmer Harris's house; and, by its dim ray, sat Harding the smuggler, watching the inanimate form of her upon whom all the strong affections of his heart had been concentrated. No persuasions could induce him to entrust "the first watch," as he called it, to others; and there he sat, seldom taking his eyes from that pale but still beautiful countenance, and often stooping over to print a kiss upon the cold and clay-like forehead of the dead. His tears were all shed: he wept not—he spoke not; but the bitterness which has no end was in his heart, and, with a sleepless eye, he watched through the livelong night. It was about three o'clock in the morning, when a hard knocking was heard at the door of the farm; and, without a change of feature, Harding rose and went down in the dark. He unlocked the door, and opened it, when a hand holding a paper was thrust in, and instantly withdrawn, as Harding took the letter.

"What is this?" he said; but the messenger ran away without reply; and the smuggler returned to the chamber of death.

The paper he had taken was folded in the shape of a note, but neither sealed nor addressed; and, without ceremony, Harding opened it, and read. It was written in a free, good hand, which he recognised at once, with rage and indignation all the more intense because he restrained them within his own breast. He uttered not a word; his face betrayed, only in part, the workings of strong passion within him. It is true, his lip quivered a little, and his brow became contracted, but it soon relaxed its frown; and, without oath or comment—though very blasphemous expletives were then tolerated in what was called the best society, and were prevalent amongst all the inferior classes,—he proceeded to read the few lines which the letter contained, and which something—perhaps the emotions he felt—had prevented him from seeing distinctly at first.

The epistle was, as we have seen, addressed to no one, and was drawn up, indeed, more in the form of a general notice than anything else. Many, of nearly the same import, as was afterwards discovered, had been delivered at various farm-houses in the neighbourhood; but, as all were in substance the same, one specimen will suffice.

"We give you to know," so the letter ran, "that, unless Edward Ramley and his two comrades are set free before daylight to-morrow, we will come to Goudhurst, and burn the place. Neither man, woman, nor child, shall escape. We are many—more than you think—and you know we will keep our word. So look to it, if you would escape—

"VENGEANCE!"

Harding approached the bed, with the letter in his hand, gazed steadfastly upon the corpse for several minutes, and then, without a word, quitted the room. He went straight to the chamber which Farmer Harris and his wife now occupied, and knocked sharply at the door, exclaiming, "Harris—Harris! I want to speak with you!"

The good farmer was with difficulty roused; for though no man felt more warmly, or, indeed, more vehemently, yet the corporeal had its full share with the mental; and when the body was fatigued with more than its ordinary portion of labour, the mind did not keep the whole being waking. At length, however, he came out, still drowsy, and taking the letter, gazed on it by the light of the candle, "with lack lustre eye!" But Harding soon brought him to active consciousness, by saying, "They threaten to burn the village, Harris, unless the murderers be suffered to escape. I am going up to the church, where they are kept.—Wake some one to sit up-stairs.—I will die before a man of them goes out."

"And so will I," cried Harris; "let me see—let me see! My heart's asleep still, but I'll soon wake up. Why, where the mischief did this come from?" and he read the letter over again, with more comprehension of its contents. When he had done, he swore vehemently, "They shall find that the men of Goudhurst can match them," he cried; "but we must set about it quick, Harding, and call up all the young men.—They will come, that is certain; for the devil himself has not their impudence; but they must be well received when they do come. We'll give them a breakfast, Harding, they shan't forget. It shall be called the Goudhurst breakfast, as long as men can remember. Stay, I'll just put on my coat, and get out the gun and the pistols—we shall want as many of those things as we can muster. I'll be back in a minute."

From that hour till five o'clock, the little village of Goudhurst was all alive. Intimation of the danger was sent to all the neighbouring farmers; every labouring man was roused from his bed with directions to meet the rest in the churchyard; and there, as the sky became grey, a busy scene was displayed, some sixty stout men being assembled before the porch, most of them armed with old muskets or fowling pieces. Amongst those to whom age or habitual authority assigned the chief place, an eager consultation went on as to their proceedings; and though there was, as is generally the case in such meetings, a great difference upon many points, yet three acts were unanimously decided upon; first, to send all the women and children out of the village—next, to despatch a messenger to Woodchurch for military aid—and, next, to set about casting bullets immediately, as no shot larger than slugs were to be found in the place.

The reader will probably ask, with a look of

surprise, "Is this a scene in North America, where settlers were daily exposed to the incursions of the savages?"—and he may add, "This could not have happened in England!" But I beg to say, this happened in the county of Kent, less than a century ago; and persons are still living, who remember having been sent with the women and children out of the village, that the men might not be impeded by fear for those they loved, while defending the spot on which they were born.

A fire of wood was speedily lighted by some of the men in the church-yard; others applied themselves, with what moulds could be procured, to the casting of ball; others, again, woke the still slumbering inhabitants of the cottages and houses round, and warned the women to remove to the neighbouring farms, and the men to come and join their friends at the rendezvous; and a few of the best instructed proceeded to arrange their plan of defence, barricading the gates of the cemetery, and blocking up a stile, which at that time led from the right hand wall, with an old grave-stone, against which they piled up a heap of earth.

The vestry, in which the prisoners had been confined—after having been brought from Mr. Broughton's at too late an hour to convey them to gaol—was luckily protected by strong iron bars over the windows, and a heavy plated door between it and the church; and the old tower of the building afforded a strong point in the position of the villagers, which they flattered themselves could not easily be forced.

"How many men do you think they can muster, Harding?" asked Farmer Harris, when their first rude preparations were nearly complete.

"I can but guess," answered the smuggler; "perhaps two hundred. They had more than that in the Marsh, of whom I hear some fifty were taken or killed; but a good many were not there, who may, and will be here to-day—old Ramley for one, I should think."

"Then we had better get into the church when they come," replied the farmer; "they cannot force us there till the soldiers come."

"Did you send for them?" asked Harding.

"Oh, yes," answered the farmer, "half-an-hour ago. I sent the young boy, who would be of no good here, on the pony; and I told *him* to let Sir Robert know, as he passed; for I thought the soldiers might not meddle if they had not a magistrate with them."

"Very well," replied Harding, and set himself to work away again.

Six o'clock was now past, seven approached and went by; the hand of the dial moved half-way on to eight, and yet nothing indicated the approach of the smugglers. In a few minutes after, however, the sound of horses' feet galloping was heard; and a young man, who had been placed in the belfry to look out, shouted down to those below, "Only two!" and the next moment a horseman in military half dress, with a servant behind him, rode up at speed to the principal entrance of the church-yard.

"I am come to help you, my men," cried Sir Edward Digby, springing to the ground, and giving his rein to his servant—"Will you let us in to your redoubt? The dragoons will soon be over; I sent your messenger on."

"Perhaps, sir, you may have your trouble for your pains, after all," answered young Harris, opening the gate, to let Digby and his horses in; "the fellows have not shown themselves, and very likely wont come."

"Oh, yes, they will," said the young baronet, advancing amongst them, and looking round on every side, "I saw a long line of men on horse-back moving over the hill as I came. Put the horses under cover of that shed, Somers. You should cut down those thick bushes near the wall. They will conceal their movements.—Have you any axes ?"

"Here is one," cried a young man, and immediately he set to work, hewing down the shrubs and bushes to which Digby pointed.

In the meantime, the young officer ran over the groups with his eye, calculating their numbers, and at length he said: "You had better confine yourselves to defending the church—you are not enough to meet them out here. I counted a hundred and fifty, and there may be more. Station your best marksmen at the windows and on the roof of the tower, and put a few stout resolute fellows to guard the door in case these scoundrels get nearer than we wish them. As we all act upon our own responsibility, however, we had better be cautious, and abstain from offensive measures, till they are absolutely necessary for the defence of ourselves and the security of the prisoners. Besides, if they are kept at bay for some time, the dragoons will take them in flank, and a good number may be captured."

"We can deal with them ourselves," said the voice of Harding, in a stern tone. He had been standing by, listening, in grave silence, with a gun in his hand, which he had borrowed at farmer Harris's; and now, as soon as he had spoken, he turned away, walked into the church, and climbed to the roof of the tower. There, after examining the priming of the piece, he seated himself coolly upon the little parapet, and looked out over the country. The moment after, his voice was heard, calling from above—"They are coming up, Harris!—Tell the officer."

Sir Edward Digby had, in the meantime, advanced to the gates to insure that they were securely fastened; but he heard what Harding said, and turning his head, exclaimed—"Go into the church; and garnish the windows with marksmen, as I said! I will be with you in a moment.—Here, Somers, help me here for a moment. They will soon pull this down;" and he proceeded calmly to fasten the barricade more strongly. Before he had accomplished this to his satisfaction, men on horseback were seen gathering thick in the road, and on the little open space in front; but he went on without pausing to look at them, till a loud voice exclaimed—"What are you about there?—Do you intend to give the men up, or not?"

Sir Edward Digby then raised his head, and replied: "Certainly not!—Oh, Mr. Richard

Radford—you will have the goodness to remark that, if you advance one step towards these gates, or attempt to pass that wall, you will be fired on from the church."

While he was speaking, he took a step back, and then walked slowly towards the building, making his servant go first; but half-way thither he paused, and turning towards the ruffians congregated at a little distance from the wall, he added aloud, addressing Richard Radford—"You had better tell your gang what I say, my good friend, for they will find we will keep our word."

As he spoke, some one from the mass fired a pistol at him; but the ball did not take effect, and Digby raised his hand, waving to those in the church not to fire, and at the same time hurrying his pace a little till he had passed the door and ordered it to be shut.

"They have now fair warning," he said to one of the young Harris's, who was on guard at the door; but I will go up above and call to you when I think anything is necessary to be done.—Remember, my good fellows, that some order must be kept; and as you cannot all be at the windows, let those who must stand back, load while the rest fire."

Thus saying, he mounted to the top of the

tower with a quick step, and found Harding and five others on the roof. The horsemen in front of the church, were all gathered together at a little distance, and seemed in eager consultation; and amongst them the figures of young Radford and the two Ramleys, father and son, were conspicuous from the vehement gestures that they made—now pointing to the top of the tower, now to the wall of the churchyard.

"I think we could bring a good many down as they stand now," said young William Harris, moving his gun towards his shoulder, as if the inclination to fire were almost irresistible.

"Stay—stay! not yet," replied Sir Edward Digby; "let it be clearly in our own defence. Besides, you must remember these are but fowling pieces. At that distance, few shots would tell."

"One shall tell, at least, before this day is over," said Harding, who had remained seated, hardly looking at the party without. "Something tells me, I shall have vengeance this day."

"Hallo! they are going to begin!" cried another man; and the same moment, the gang of miscreants spread out, and while some advanced on horseback towards the wall, at least fifty, who were armed with guns, dismounted and aimed deliberately at the tower and the windows.

"Down with your heads behind the parapet!" cried Digby, though he did not follow the caution himself; "no use of exposing your lives needlessly. Down—down, Harding!"

But Harding sat where he was, saying, bitterly, "They'll not hit me.—I know it—they've done worse already." As he spoke, a single gun was fired, and then a volley, from the two sides of the churchyard wall. One of the balls whizzed close by Sir Edward Digby's head, and another struck the parapet near Harding; but neither were touched, and the stout seaman did not move a muscle.

"Now up, and give it them back!" exclaimed Digby; and, speaking down the trap that led to the stairs, he called to those below, "Fire now, and pick them off!—Steadily—steadily!" he continued, addressing his companions on the roof, who were becoming somewhat too much excited. "Make every shot tell, if you can—a good aim—a good aim!"

"Here goes for one!" cried William Harris, aiming at Jim Ramley, and hitting him in the thigh; and instantly, from the roof and the windows of the church, blazed forth a sharp fire of musketry, which apparently was not without severe effect; for the men who had dismounted were thrown into great confusion, and the horsemen who were advancing recoiled, with several of their horses plunging violently.

The only one on the roof who did not fire was Harding, and he remained with his gun resting on the parapet beside him, gazing, with a stern, dark brow, upon the scene.

"There are three down," cried one of the men, "and a lot of horses!"

But Richard Radford was seen gesticulating vehemently; and at length taking off his hat, he waved it in the air, shouting, so loud that his words reached those above, "I will show you the way, then; let every brave man follow me!" And as he spoke he struck his spurs into his horse's sides, galloped on, and pushed his beast at the low wall of the churchyard.

The animal, a powerful hunter, which had been sent to him by his father the day before, rose to the leap as if with pride. But just then, Harding raised his gun, aimed steadily, and pulled the trigger. The smoke for a moment obscured Digby's view; but the instant after he saw Richard Radford falling headlong from the saddle, and his shoulder striking the wall as the horse cleared it. The body then fell over, bent up, with the head leaning against a tombstone and the legs upon an adjoining grave.

"There!—that's done!" said Harding; and laying down the gun again, he betook himself quietly to his seat upon the parapet once more.

"The dragoons! the dragoons!" cried a young man from the other side of the tower. But ere he spoke, the gang of villains were already in retreat, several galloping away, and the rest wavering.

Loading as fast as they could, the stout yeomanry in the church continued firing from the windows and from the roof, accelerating the movements of their assailants, who seemed only to pause for the purpose of carrying off their wounded companions. Sir Edward Digby, however, ran round to the opposite side of the tower, and, clearly seeing the advance of some cavalry from the side of Cranbrook—though the trees prevented him from ascertaining their numbers—he bade the rest follow, and ran down into the body of the church.

"Now out, and after them!" he exclaimed; "we may make some prisoners!" But as soon as the large wooden doors were thrown back and the peasantry were seen pouring forth, old Ramley, who was amongst the last that lingered, turned his horse and galloped away, his companions following as fast as they could. Four men were found on the outside of the churchyard wall, of whom two were living; but Sir Edward Digby advanced with several others to the spot where Richard Radford was lying. He did not appear to have moved at all since he fell; and on raising his head, which had fallen forward on his chest as he lay propped up by the grave-stone, a dark red spot in the centre of the fore-head, from which a small quantity of blood had flowed down over his eyes and cheeks, told how fatally true the shot had gone to the mark.

When he had gazed on him for a moment, Digby turned round again, to look for Harding; but the man who had slain him, did not approach the corpse of Richard Radford; and Digby perceived him standing near a low shed, which at that time encumbered the churchyard of Goudhurst, and under which the young baronet's horses had been placed. Thither the strong hunter, which Radford had been riding, had trotted as soon as his master fell; and Harding had caught it by the bridle, and was gazing at it with a thoughtful look.

The last time Sir Edward Digby had seen him, before that morning, he was in high happiness by the side of poor Kate Clare; and when the young officer looked at him, as he stood there, with a sort of dull despair in his whole aspect, he could not but feel strong and painful sympathy with him, in his deep grief.

"Mr. Harding," he said, approaching him, "the unhappy man is quite dead."

"Oh, yes, sir," answered Harding, "dead enough, I am sure. I hope he knew whose hand did it."

"I am sorry to give you any further pain or anxiety, at this moment," continued Digby, sinking his voice, "but I have heard that you are supposed to have taken some part in landing the goods which were captured the other day. For aught we know, there may be information lodged against you; and probably there will be some officer of Customs with the troop that is coming up. Would it not be better for you to retire from this scene for a little?"

"Thank you, sir,—thank you! That is kind!" answered Harding. "Life's a load to me; but a prison is another thing. I would have given any of those clumsy fellows a hundred guineas to have shot me as I sat there but no man shall ever take me, and clap me up in a cell. I could not bear that; and my poor Kate lying dead there, too!—I'll go, as you say."

But before he could execute his purpose, a small party of dragoons, commanded by a lieutenant, with Birchett, the riding officer, and two or three of his companions, came up at a trot, and poured through the gate of the churchyard, which was now open.

Sir Edward Digby advanced at once towards them — if the truth must be told, to cover Harding's retreat; but Birchett's quick, shrewd eye had run round the place in an instant; and, before the young baronet had taken two steps along the path, he cried, "Why, there is Harding! Stop him! — stop him! We have information against him. Don't let him pass!"

"I *will* pass, though," cried Harding, leaping at once upon the back of Richard Radford's horse. "Now, stop me if you can!" and striking it with his heel, he turned the animal across the churchyard, taking an angle, away from the dragoons. Birchett spurred after him in a moment; and the other officers followed; but the soldiers did not move. Passing close by the spot where young Radford lay, as the officers tried to cut him off from the gate,

Harding cried, with a wild and bitter laugh, "He is a good leaper, I know!" and instantly pushed his horse at the wall.

The gallant beast took it at once, and dashed away with its rider along the road. The officers of Customs dared not trust their own cattle with the same feat; but Birchett exclaimed, in a loud and imperative tone, turning to the lieutenant of dragoons, "I require your aid in capturing that man. He is one of the most daring smugglers on the whole coast. We can catch him easily, if we are quick."

"I do not know that I am authorized," said the lieutenant, not well pleased with the man's manner; "where no armed resistance is apprehended, I doubt if——"

"But there may be resistance, sir," replied Birchett, vehemently; "he is gone to join his comrades.—Well, the responsibility be on your head! I claim your aid! Refuse it or not, as you shall think fit.—I claim and require it instantly!"

"What do you think, sir?" asked the young officer, turning to Digby.

"Nay, I am not in command here," answered the other; "you know your orders."

"To give all lawful aid and assistance," said

the lieutenant. "Well, take a serjeant's guard, Mr. Birchett."

In haste, the men were drawn out, and followed: Birchett leading them furiously on the pursuit; but ere they had quitted the churchyard, Harding was half-a-mile upon the road; and that was all he desired.

CHAPTER XIII.

There was a large lugger lying off, at no great distance from the beach, near Sandgate, and a small boat, ready for launching, on the shore. At the distance of two or three miles out, might be seen a vessel of considerable size, and of that peculiar rig and build which denoted, to nautical eyes, that there lay a king's vessel. She was, indeed, a frigate of inferior class, which had been sent round to co-operate with the Customs, in the suppression of the daring system of smuggling, which, as we have shown, was carried on in Romney Marsh, and the neighbouring country. By the lesser boat, upon the shore, stood four stout fellows, apparently employed in making ready to put off; and upon the high ground above, was seen a single officer of Customs, walking carelessly to and fro, and apparently taking little heed of the proceedings below. Some movements might be perceived on board the ship; the sails, which had been furled, now began to flutter in the wind, which was blowing strong; and it seemed evident that the little frigate was about to get under weigh. The lugger, however, remained stationary; and the men near the boat continued their labours for nearly an hour after they seemed in reality to have nothing more to do.

At length, however, coming at a furious pace, down one of the narrow foot-paths from the high ground above, which led away towards Cheriton and Newington, was seen a horseman, waving his hand to those below, and passing within fifty yards of the officer of Customs. The sailors, who were standing by the boat, instantly pushed her down to the very verge of the water; the officer hallooed after the bold rider, but without causing him to pause for an instant in his course; and down, at thundering speed, across the road, and over the sand and shingle, Harding, the smuggler, dashed on, till the horse that bore him stood foaming and panting beside the boat. Instantly springing out of the saddle, he cast the bridle on the tired beast's neck, and jumped into the skiff, exclaiming, "Shove her off!"

"Arn't there some more, Jack?" asked one of the men.

"None but myself," replied Harding, "and me they shan't catch.—Shove her off, I say—you'll soon see who are coming after!"

The men obeyed at once; the boat was launched into the water; and almost at the same instant, the party of dragoons in pursuit appeared upon the top of the rise, followed, a moment after, by Birchett, and another officer of the Customs. The vehement and angry gestures of the riding officer indicated plainly enough that he saw the prey had escaped him; but while the dragoons and his fellow officer made their way slowly down the bank, to the narrow road which at that time ran along the beach, he galloped off towards a signal-post, which then stood upon an elevated spot, not far from the place where the turnpike, on the road between Sandgate and Folkestone, now stands. In a few minutes various small flags were seen rapidly running up to the top of the staff; and, as speedily as possible afterwards, signals of the same kind were displayed on board the frigate.

In the meantime, however, Harding and his

party had rowed rapidly towards the lugger, the sails of which were already beginning to fill; and in less than two minutes she was scudding through the water as fast as the wind would bear her. But the frigate was also under weigh; and, to both experienced and inexperienced eyes, it seemed that the bold smuggler had hardly one chance of escape. Between Dungeness Point, and the royal vessel, there appeared to be no space for any of those daring manœuvres by which the small vessels, engaged in the contraband trade, occasionally eluded the pursuit of their larger and more formidable opponents; but Harding still pursued his course, striving to get into the open sea, before the frigate could cut him off.

Bending under the press of sail, the boat rushed through the waves, with the uptide running strong against her, and the spray dashing over her from stem to stern; but still, as she took an angle, though an acute one, with the course of the frigate, the latter gained upon her every moment, till at length a shot, whistling across her bows, gave her the signal to bring to. It is needless to tell the reader, that signal received no attention; but, still steered with a firm hand, and carrying every stitch of canvas she could bear, the lugger pursued her way. A minute had scarcely passed, ere flash and report came again from the frigate, and once more a ball whistled by. Another and another followed; but, no longer directed across the lugger's bows, they were evidently aimed directly at her; and one of them passed through the foresail, though without doing any farther damage. The case seemed so hopeless, not only to those who watched the whole proceeding from the shore, but to most of those who were in the lugger, that a murmured consultation took place among the men; and after two or three more shots had been fired, coming each time nearer and nearer to their flying mark, one of the crew turned to Harding, who had scarcely uttered a word since he entered the boat, and said, "Come, sir, I don't think this will do.—We shall only get ourselves sunk for no good.—We had better douse."

Harding looked sternly at him for a moment without reply; and a somewhat bitter answer rose to his lips. But he checked himself, and said, at length, "There's no use sacrificing your lives. You've got wives and children—fathers and mothers. I have no one to care for me.—Get into the boat, and be off. Me they shall never catch, dead or alive; and if I go to the bottom, it's the best berth for me now.

Here, just help me reeve these tiller-ropes that I may take shelter under the companion; and then be off as fast as you can."

The men would fain have remonstrated; but Harding would hear nothing; and, covering himself as much as he could from the aim of small arms from the vessel, he insisted that the whole of his crew should go and leave him.

A short pause in the lugger's flight was observable from the shore; and everybody concluded that she had struck. The row-boat, filled with men, was seen to pull off from her, and the large heavy sails to flap for an instant in the wind. But then her course was altered in a moment; the sails filled again with the full breeze; and going like a swallow over the waves, she dashed on towards the frigate, and, passing her within pistol-range immediately after, shot across upon her weather-bow.

A cloud of smoke ran all along the side of the frigate, as this bold and extraordinary manœuvre was executed. The faint report of small arms was wafted by the wind to the shore, as well as the sound of several cannon; but still, whether Harding was wounded or not wounded, living or dead, his gallant boat dashed steadily on, and left the frigate far behind, apparently giving up the chase, as no longer presenting any chance of success. On, on, went the lugger, diminishing as it flew over the waves, till at length, to the eyes even of those who watched from the heights, its dark, tanned sails grouped themselves into one small speck, and were then lost to the sight.

The after-fate of that adventurous man, who thus, single and unaided, trusted himself to the wide waves, is wrapped in obscurity. The writer of these pages, indeed, did once see a stern-looking old man of the same name, who had returned some few years before from distant lands—no one well knew whence—to spend the last few years of a life, which had been protracted considerably beyond the ordinary term of human existence, in a seaport not very far from Folkestone. The conversation of the people of the place pointed him out as one who had done extraordinary deeds, and seen strange sights; but whether he was, indeed, the Harding of this tale or not, I cannot say. Of one thing, however, the reader may be certain, that in all the statements regarding the smuggler's marvellous escape, the most scrupulous accuracy has been observed, and that every fact is as true as any part of history, and a great deal more so than most.

Having now disposed of one of our principal

characters, let me take the reader gently by the hand, and lead him back to Harbourne House. The way is somewhat long, but still, not more than a stout man can walk without fatigue upon a pleasant morning; and it lies, too, amongst sweet and interesting scenes—which, to you and me, dear reader, are, I trust, embellished by some of the charms of association.

It was about six days after the attack, upon the church at Goudhurst, when a great number of those personages with whom it has been necessary to make the reader acquainted, were assembled in the drawing-room of Sir Robert Croyland's mansion. One or two, indeed, were wanting, even of the party which might have been expected there, but their absence shall be accounted for hereafter. The baronet himself was seated in the arm-chair, which he generally occupied more as a mark of his state and dignity, than for comfort and convenience. In the present instance, however, he seemed to need support, for he leaned heavily upon the arm of the chair, and appeared languid and feeble. His face was very pale, his lips somewhat livid; and yet, though suffering evidently under considerable corporeal debility, there was a look of mental relief in his eyes, and a sweet placidity about his smile, that no one had seen on his countenance for many years.

Mrs. Barbara was, as usual, seated at her everlasting embroidery; and here we may as well mention a fact which we omitted to mention before, but which some persons may look upon as indicative of her mental character—namely, that the embroidery, though it had gone on all her life, by no means proceeded in an even course of progression. On the contrary, to inexperienced eyes, it seemed as if no sooner was a stitch put in than it was drawn out again, the point of the needle being gently thrust under the loop of the thread, and then the arm extended with an even sweep, so as to withdraw the silk from its hole in the canvas. Penelope's web was nothing to Mrs. Barbary Croyland's embroidery; for the queen of Ithaca only undid what she had previously done, every night; and Aunt Bab undid it every minute. On the present occasion, she was more busy in the retroactive process than ever, not only pulling out the silk she had just put in, but a great deal more; so that the work of the last three days, was in imminent danger of total destruction.

Mr. Zachary Croyland never sat down when he could stand; for there was about him, a sort of mobility and activity of spirits, which always inclined him to keep his body ready for action. He so well knew that, when seated, he was incessantly inclined to start up again, that probably he thought it of little use to sit down at all; and consequently he was even now upon his feet, midway between his brother and his sister, rubbing his hands, and giving a gay, but cynical glance from one to the other.

In a chair near the window, with his wild, but fine eye gazing over the pleasant prospect which the terrace commanded, and apparently altogether absent in mind from the scene in the drawing-room, was seated Mr. Osborn; and not far from Mr. Croyland stood Sir Henry Leyton, in an ordinary riding-dress, with his left hand resting on the hilt of his sword, speaking in an easy, quiet tone to Sir Robert Croyland; and nearly opposite to him was Edith, with her arm resting on the table, and her cheek supported on her hand. Her face was still pale, though the colour had somewhat returned; and the expression was grave, though calm. Indeed, she never recovered the gay and sparkling look which had characterized her countenance in early youth; but the expression had gained in depth and intensity more than it had lost in brightness; and then, when she did smile, it was with ineffable sweetness: a gleam of sunshine upon the deep sea. Her eyes were fixed upon her lover; and those who knew her well could read in them satisfaction, love, hope—nay, more than hope—a pride, the only pride that she could know—that he whom she had chosen in her girlhood, to whom she had remained true and faithful through years of sorrow and unexampled trial, had proved himself in every way worthy of her first affection and her long constancy.

But where was Zara?—where Sir Edward Digby? for neither of them were present at the time. From the laws of attraction between different terrestrial bodies, we have every reason to infer that Digby and Zara were not very far apart. However, they had been somewhat eccentric in their orbits; for Zara had gone out about a couple of hours before—Digby being then absent, no one knew where—upon a charitable errand, to carry consolation and sympathy to the cottage of poor Mrs. Clare, whose daughter had been committed to the earth the day before. How it happened, Heaven only knows, but certain it is, that at the moment I now speak of, she and Digby were walking home together, towards

Harbourne House, while his servant led his horse at some distance behind.

Before they reached the house, however, a long conversation had taken place between the personages in the drawing-room, of which I shall only give the last few sentences.

"It is true, Harry, it is true," said Sir Robert Croyland, in reply to something just spoken by Leyton; "and we have both things to forgive; but you far more than I have; and as you have set me an example of doing good for evil, and atoning, by every means, for a slight error, I will not be backward to do the same, and to acknowledge that I have acted most wrongly towards you—for which may Heaven forgive me, as you have done. I have small means of atoning for much that is past; but to do so, as far as possible: freely, and with my full consent, take the most valuable thing I have to give—my dear child's hand,—nay, hear me yet a moment. I wish your marriage to take place as soon as possible. I have learned to doubt of time, and never to trust the future. Say a week—a fortnight, Edith; but let it be speedily. It is my wish—let me say, for the last time, it is my command."

"But, brother Robert," exclaimed Mrs. Barbara, ruining her embroidery irretrievably in the agitation of the moment, "you know it can't be so very soon; for there are all the dresses to get ready, and the settlements to be drawn up, and a thousand things to buy; and our cousins in Yorkshire must be informed, and——"

"D—n our cousins in Yorkshire!" exclaimed Mr. Zachary Croyland. "Now, my dear Bab, tell me candidly, whether you have or have not any nice little plan ready for spoiling the whole, and throwing us all into confusion again. Don't you think you could just send Edith to visit somebody in the small-pox? or get Harry Leyton run through in a duel? or some other little comfortable consummation, which may make us all as unhappy as possible?"

"Really, brother Zachary, I don't know what you mean," said Mrs. Barbara, looking the picture of injured innocence.

"I dare say not, Bab," answered Mr. Croyland; "but I understand what you mean; and I tell you it shall not be. Edith shall fix the day; and as a good child, she will obey her father, and fix it as early as possible. When once fixed, it shall not be changed or put off, on any account or consideration whatever, if my name's Croyland. As for the dresses, don't you trouble your head about that; I'll undertake the dresses, and have them all down from

London by the coach. Give me the size of your waist, Edith, upon a piece of string, and your length from shoulder to heel, and leave all the rest to me. If I don't dress her like a Mahommedan princess, may I never hear *Bismillah* again."

Edith smiled, but answered, "I don't think it will be at all necessary, my dear uncle, to put you to the trouble; and I do not think it would answer its purpose if you took it."

"But I will have my own way," said Mr. Croyland—"you are my pet; and all the matrimonial arrangements shall be mine. If you don't mind, and say another word, I'll insist upon being bridesmaid too; for I can encroach in my demands, I can tell you, as well as a lady, or a prime minister."

As he spoke, the farther progress of the discussion was interrupted by the entrance of Zara, followed by Sir Edward Digby. Her colour was a little heightened, and her manner somewhat agitated; but she shook hands with her uncle and Leyton, neither of whom she had seen before during that morning; and then passing by her father, in her way towards Edith, she whispered a word to him as she went.

"What, what!" exclaimed Sir Robert Croyland, turning suddenly round towards Digby, with a look of alarm, and pressing his left hand upon his side, "she says you have something important to tell me, Sir Edward.—Pray speak! I have no secrets from those who are around me."

"I am sure, what I have to say will shock all present!" replied Sir Edward Digby, gravely; "but the fact is, I heard a report this morning, from my servant, that Mr. Radford had destroyed himself last night in prison; and I rode over as fast as I could, to ascertain if the rumour was correct. I found that it was but too accurate, and that the unhappy man terminated a career of crime, by the greatest that he could commit."

"Well, there's one rascal less in the world—that's some comfort," said Mr. Zachary Croyland; "I would rather, indeed, he had let some one else hang him, instead of doing it himself; for I don't approve of suicide at all—it's foolish, and wicked, and cowardly. Still, nothing else could be expected from such a man—but what's the matter with you, Robert? you seem ill—surely, you can't take this man's death much to heart?"

Sir Robert Croyland did not reply, but made

a faint sign to open the window, which was immediately done; and he revived under the influence of the air.

"I will go out for a few minutes," he said, rising; and Edith, instantly starting up, approached to go with him. He would not suffer her, however—"No, my child," he replied to her offer, "no: you can understand what I feel; but I shall be better presently. Stay here, and let all this be settled; and remember, Edith, name the earliest day possible—arrange with Zara and Digby. Theirs can take place at the same time."

Thus saying, he went out, and was seen walking slowly to and fro upon the terrace, for some minutes after. In the meanwhile, the war had commenced between Mr. Zachary Croyland and his younger niece. "Ah, Mrs. Madcap!" he exclaimed, "so I hear tales of you. The coquette has been caught at length! You are going to commit matrimony; and as birds of a feather flock together, the wild girl and the wild boy must pair."

With her usual light, graceful step, and with her usual gay and brilliant smile, Zara left Sir Edward Digby's side, and crossing over to her uncle, rested both her hands upon his arm, while he stood as erect and stiff as a finger post, gazing down upon her with a look of sour fun. But in Zara's eyes, beautiful and beaming as they were, there was a look of deeper feeling than they usually displayed when jesting, as was her wont, with Mr. Croyland.

"Well, Chit," he said, "well, what do you want ?—a new gown, or a smart hat, or a riding-whip, with a tiger's head in gold at the top ?"

"No, my dear uncle," she answered, "but I want you not to tease me, nor to laugh at me, nor to abuse me, just now. For once in my life, I feel that I must be serious; and I think even less teasing than ordinary might be too much for me. Perhaps, one time or another, you may find out that poor Zara's coquetry was more apparent than real, and that though she had an object, it was a better one than you, in your benevolence, were disposed to think."

An unwonted drop swam in her eyes as she spoke; and Mr. Croyland gazed down upon her tenderly for a moment. Then throwing his arms round her, he kissed her cheek—"I know it, my dear," he said—"I know it. Edith has told me all; and she who has been a kind, good sister, will, I am sure, be a kind, good wife. Here, take her away, Digby. A better girl doesn't live, whatever I may have said. The worst of it is, she is a great deal too good for you, or any other wild, harem-scarem fellow. But stay—stay," he continued, as Digby came forward, laughing, and took Zara's hand; "here's something with her; for, as I am sure you will be a couple of spendthrifts, it is but fit that you should have something to set out upon."

Mr. Croyland, as he spoke, put his hand into the somewhat wide and yawning pocket of his broad-tailed coat, and produced his pocket-book; from which he drew forth a small slip of paper.

Digby took it, and looked at it, but instantly held it out again to Mr. Croyland, saying, "My dear sir, it is quite unnecessary. I claim nothing but her hand; and that is mine by promises which I hope will not be very long ere they are fulfilled."

"Nonsense, nonsense!" cried Mr. Croyland, putting away the paper with the back of his hand; "did ever any one see such a fool?—I tell you, Sir Edward Digby, I'm as proud a man as you are; and you shall not marry my niece without receiving the same portion as her sister possesses. I hate all eldest sons, as you well know; and I don't see why eldest daughters should exist either. I'll have them all equal.

No differences here. I've made up to Zara, the disparity which one fool of an uncle thought fit to put between her and Edith. Such was always my intention; and moreover, let it clearly be understood, that when you have put this old carrion under ground, what I leave is to be divided between them—all equal, all equal—co-heiresses, of Zachary Croyland, Esq., surnamed the Nabob, alias the Misanthrope—and then, if you like it, you may each bear in your arms a crow rampant, on an escutcheon of pretence."

"Thank you, thank you, my dear uncle," answered Edith Croyland, while Zara's gay heart was too full to let her speak—"thank you for such thought of my sweet sister; for, indeed, to me, during long years of sorrow and trouble, she has been the spirit of consolation, comfort, strength—even hope."

Poor Zara was overpowered; and she burst into tears. It seemed as if all the feelings, which for the sake of others she had so long suppressed—all the emotions, anxieties, and cares which she had conquered or treated lightly, in order to give aid and support to Edith, rushed upon her at once in the moment of joy, and overwhelmed her.

"Why, what's the foolish girl crying about?"

exclaimed Mr. Croyland; but then, drawing her kindly to him, he added, " Come, my dear, we will make a truce, upon the following conditions —I wont tease you any more; and you shall do everything I tell you. In the first place, then, wipe your eyes, and dry up your tears; for if Digby sees how red your cheeks can look, when you've been crying, he may find out that you are not quite such a Venus as he fancies just now— There, go along!" and he pushed her gently away from him.

While this gayer conversation had been going on within, Mr. Osborn had passed through the glass doors, and was walking slowly up and down with Sir Robert Croyland. The subject they spoke upon must have been grave; for there was gloom upon both their faces when they returned.

"I know it," said Sir Robert Croyland to his companion as they entered the room; "I am quite well aware of it; it is that which makes me urge speed."

"If such be your view," replied Mr. Osborn, "you are right, Sir Robert; and Heaven bless those acts, which are done under such impressions."

The party in the drawing-room heard no

more; and, notwitstanding the kindly efforts of Mrs. Barbara, and a thousand little impediments, which, "with the very best motives in the world," she created or discovered, all the arrangements for the double marriage were made with great promptitude and success. At the end of somewhat less than a fortnight, without any noise or parade, the two sisters stood together at the altar, and pledged their troth to those they truly loved. Sir Robert Croyland seemed well and happy; for during the last few days previous to the wedding, both his health and spirits had apparently improved. But, ere a month was over, both his daughters received a summons to return, as speedily as possible, to Harbourne House. They found him on the bed of death, with his brother and Mr. Osborn sitting beside him. But their father greeted them with a well-contented smile, and reproved their tears in a very different tone from that which he had been generally accustomed to use.

"My dear children," he said, in a feeble voice, "I have often longed for this hour; and though life has become happier now, I have, for many weeks, seen death approaching, and have seen it without regret. I did not think it would have been so slow; and that was the cause of my hurrying your marriage; for I longed to witness it with my own eyes, yet was unwilling to mingle the happiness of such a union, with the thought that it took place while I was in sickness and danger. My brother will be a father to you, I am sure, when I am gone; but still it is some satisfaction to know that you have both better protectors, even here on earth, than he or I could be. I trust you are happy; and believe me, I am not otherwise—though lying here with death before me."

Towards four o'clock on the following day, the windows of Harbourne House were closed; and, about a week after, the mortal remains of Sir Robert Croyland were conveyed to the family vault in the village church. Mr. Croyland succeeded to the estates and title of his brother; but he would not quit the mansion which he himself had built, leaving Mrs. Barbara, with a handsome income, which he secured to her, to act the Lady Bountiful of Harbourne House.

The fate of Edith and Zara we need not farther trace. It was such as might be expected from the circumstances in which they were now placed. We will not venture to say that it was purely happy; for when was ever pure and unalloyed happiness found on earth?

There were cares, there were anxieties, there were griefs, from time to time: for the splendid visions of young imagination may be prophetic of joys that *shall* be ours, if we deserve them in our trial here, but are never realized within the walls of our mortal prison, and recede before us, to take their stand for ever beyond the portals of the tomb. But still they were as happy as human beings, perhaps, ever were; for no peculiar pangs or sufferings were destined to follow those which had gone before; and in their domestic life, having chosen well and wisely, they found—as every one will find, who judges upon such grounds—that love, when it is pure, and high, and true, is a possession, to the brightness of which even hope can add no sweetness, imagination no splendour that it does not in itself possess.

The reader may be inclined to ask the after fate of some of the other characters mentioned in this work. In regard to many of them, I must give an unsatisfactory reply. What became of most, indeed, I do not know. The name of Mowle, the officer of Customs, is still familiar to the people of Hythe and its neighbourhood. It is certain that Ramley and one of his sons were hanged; but the rest of the records of that respectable family are, I fear, lost to the public. Little Starlight seems to have disappeared from that part of the country, for some time; and in truth, I have no certainty that the well-known pickpocket, Night Ray, who was transported to Botany Bay, some thirty years after the period of this tale, and was shot in an attempt to escape, was the same person whose early career is here recorded. But of one thing the reader may be perfectly certain, that—whatever was the fortune which attended any of the persons I have mentioned—whether worldly prosperity, or temporary adversity befel them—the real, the solid good, the happiness of spirit, was awarded in exact proportion to each, as their acts were good, and their hearts were pure.

THE END.

T. C. Savill, Printer, 4, Chandos Street, Covent Garden.

CPSIA information can be obtained
at www.ICGtesting.com
Printed in the USA
BVHW011040190622
640128BV00003B/50